3rd Edition

Ventures

Basic

STUDENT'S BOOK

Gretchen Bitterlin ▪ **Dennis Johnson** ▪ **Donna Price** ▪ **Sylvia Ramirez**

K. Lynn Savage (Series Editor)

CAMBRIDGE
UNIVERSITY PRESS

CAMBRIDGE
UNIVERSITY PRESS

University Printing House, Cambridge CB2 8BS, United Kingdom

One Liberty Plaza, 20th Floor, New York, NY 10006, USA

477 Williamstown Road, Port Melbourne, VIC 3207, Australia

314–321, 3rd Floor, Plot 3, Splendor Forum, Jasola District Centre, New Delhi – 110025, India

79 Anson Road, #06–04/06, Singapore 079906

Cambridge University Press is part of the University of Cambridge.

It furthers the University's mission by disseminating knowledge in the pursuit of education, learning and research at the highest international levels of excellence.

www.cambridge.org
Information on this title: www.cambridge.org/9781108449533

© Cambridge University Press 2018

This publication is in copyright. Subject to statutory exception and to the provisions of relevant collective licensing agreements, no reproduction of any part may take place without the written permission of Cambridge University Press.

First published 2008
Second edition 2014

20 19 18 17 16 15 14 13 12 11 10 9 8 7 6

Printed in Malaysia by Vivar Printing

A catalogue record for this publication is available from the British Library

ISBN 978-1-108-44998-4 Workbook
ISBN 978-1-108-44966-3 Literacy Workbook
ISBN 978-1-108-44932-8 Online Workbook
ISBN 978-1-108-57321-4 Teacher's Edition
ISBN 978-1-108-44919-9 Class Audio CDs
ISBN 978-1-108-45027-0 Presentation Plus

Additional resources for this publication at www.cambridge.org/ventures

Cambridge University Press has no responsibility for the persistence or accuracy of URLs for external or third-party internet websites referred to in this publication, and does not guarantee that any content on such websites is, or will remain, accurate or appropriate. Information regarding prices, travel timetables, and other factual information given in this work is correct at the time of first printing but Cambridge University Press does not guarantee the accuracy of such information thereafter.

AUTHORS' ACKNOWLEDGMENTS

The authors would like to acknowledge and thank focus-group participants and reviewers for their insightful comments, as well as Cambridge University Press editorial, marketing, and production staffs, whose thorough research and attention to detail have resulted in a quality product.

The publishers would also like to extend their particular thanks to the following reviewers and consultants for their valuable insights and suggestions:

Barry Bakin, Instructional Technology, Los Angeles Unified School District, Los Angeles, CA;

Jim Brice, San Diego Community College District Continuing Education, San Diego, CA;

Diana Contreras, West Valley Occupational Center, Los Angeles, CA;

Druci J. Diaz, Hillsborough Country Public Schools, Tampa, FL;

Linda Foster, Instructor, Hillsborough County Schools Adult Education Department, Tampa, FL;

Margaret Geiger, M.Ed., Dallas, TX;

Ana L. Herrera, San Jacinto Adult Learning Center, El Paso, TX;

Cindi Hartmen, ESL Instructor, San Diego Continuing Education, San Diego, CA;

Patrick Jennings, Tomlinson Adult Learning Center, St. Petersburg, FL;

Lori Hess-Tolbert, Frisco, TX;

AnnMarie Kokash-Wood, Tomlinson Adult Learning Center, St. Petersburg, FL;

Linda P. Kozin, San Diego Continuing Ed, San Diego Community College District, San Diego, CA;

Caron Lieber, Palomar College, San Marcos, CA;

Reyna P. Lopez, Southwest College, Los Angeles, CA;

Rosemary Lubarov, Palo Alto Adult School, Palo Alto, CA;

Lori K. Markel, Plant City Adult and Community School, Plant City, FL;

Mary Spanarke, Center for Applied Linguistics / Washington English Center, Washington, DC;

Rosalie Tauscher, Fort Worth ISD Adult Ed, Fort Worth, TX;

Timothy Wahl, Abram Friedman Occupation Center, Los Angeles, CA;

Delia Watley, Irving ISD Adult Education and Literacy, Irving, TX;

Andrea V. White, Tarrant County College, Arlington, TX;

Sandra Wilson, Fort Worth Adult Education, Fort Worth, TX

SCOPE AND SEQUENCE

UNIT TITLE TOPIC	FUNCTIONS	LISTENING AND SPEAKING	VOCABULARY	GRAMMAR FOCUS
Welcome pages 2–5	■ Identifying the letters of the alphabet ■ Spelling names ■ Identifying classroom directions ■ Identifying numbers	■ Saying classroom directions ■ Saying the alphabet ■ Saying numbers	■ Classroom directions ■ The alphabet with capital and lowercase letters ■ Numbers	
Unit 1 **Personal information** pages 6–17 Topic: **Describing people**	■ Identifying names ■ Identifying area codes and phone numbers ■ Identifying countries of origin ■ Exchanging personal information	■ Asking and answering questions about personal information	■ Personal information ■ Countries ■ Months of the year	■ Possessive adjectives (*my, your, his, her*)
Unit 2 **At school** pages 18–29 Topic: **The classroom**	■ Identifying classroom objects ■ Describing location ■ Finding out location	■ Asking what someone needs ■ Asking about and giving the location of things	■ Classroom furniture ■ Classroom objects ■ Days of the week	■ Prepositions of location (*in, on, under*)
Review: Units 1 and 2 pages 30–31		■ Understanding conversations		
Unit 3 **Friends and family** pages 32–43 Topic: **Family**	■ Identifying family relationships ■ Describing a family picture	■ Asking and answering questions about family relationships	■ Family relationships ■ Family members ■ People	■ *Yes / No* questions with *have*
Unit 4 **Health** pages 44–55 Topic: **Health problems**	■ Describing health problems	■ Asking and answering questions about health problems	■ The doctor's office ■ Body parts ■ Health problems	■ Singular and plural nouns
Review: Units 3 and 4 pages 56–57		■ Understanding conversations		
Unit 5 **Around town** pages 58–69 Topic: **Places and locations**	■ Identifying buildings and places ■ Describing location	■ Asking and answering questions about where someone is ■ Asking and answering questions about the location of buildings and places ■ Describing your neighborhood	■ Buildings and places ■ Transportation	■ Prepositions of location (*on, next to, across from, between*) ■ *Where* questions

READING	WRITING	LIFE SKILLS	PRONUNCIATION
■ Reading classroom directions ■ Reading the alphabet ■ Reading numbers	■ Writing the alphabet ■ Writing numbers	■ Understanding classroom directions	■ Pronouncing the alphabet ■ Pronouncing numbers
■ Reading a paragraph about a new student	■ Completing sentences giving personal information ■ Completing an ID card	■ Reading an ID card	■ Pronouncing key vocabulary ■ Pronouncing area codes and phone numbers
■ Reading a note about school supplies ■ Reading a memo about class information	■ Completing sentences about class information	■ Reading a class schedule	■ Pronouncing key vocabulary
			■ Pronouncing a as in *name* and o as in *phone*
■ Reading a paragraph about a family	■ Completing sentences about a family ■ Completing sentences about your family	■ Reading a housing application	■ Pronouncing key vocabulary
■ Reading a paragraph about a visit to the doctor's office	■ Completing a sign-in sheet at the doctor's office	■ Reading a label on a box of medicine	■ Pronouncing key vocabulary
			■ Pronouncing e as in *read*, i as in *five*, and u as in *June*
■ Reading a notice about a library opening ■ Reading a description of someone's street	■ Completing sentences describing your street	■ Reading a map	■ Pronouncing key vocabulary

UNIT TITLE TOPIC	FUNCTIONS	LISTENING AND SPEAKING	VOCABULARY	GRAMMAR FOCUS
Unit 6 Time pages 70–81 Topic: **Daily activities and time**	■ Asking the time ■ Asking for and giving information about the days and times of events	■ Asking and answering questions about the time ■ Asking and answering questions about events	■ Clock time ■ Activities and events ■ Times of the day	■ *Yes / No* questions with *be*
Review: Units 5 and 6 pages 82–83		■ Understanding conversations		
Unit 7 Shopping pages 84–95 Topic: **Clothes and prices**	■ Identifying clothing items ■ Reading prices ■ Identifying colors	■ Asking and answering questions about prices ■ Identifying the colors of clothing	■ Clothing ■ Prices ■ Colors	■ *How much is? / How much are?*
Unit 8 Work pages 96–107 Topic: **Jobs and skills**	■ Identifying jobs ■ Identifying job duties	■ Asking and answering questions about jobs ■ Asking and answering questions about job duties	■ Names of jobs ■ Job duties	■ *Yes / No* questions with simple present ■ Short answers with *does* and *doesn't*
Review: Units 7 and 8 pages 108–109		■ Understanding conversations		
Unit 9 Daily living pages 110–121 Topic: **Home responsibilities**	■ Identifying family chores	■ Asking and answering questions about family chores ■ Asking and answering questions about people's activities	■ Chores ■ Rooms of a house	■ *What* questions with the present continuous
Unit 10 Free time pages 122–133 Topic: **Free time**	■ Identifying free-time activities ■ Describing what people like to do	■ Asking and answering questions about free-time activities	■ Free-time activities	■ *like to* + verb ■ *What* questions with *like to* + verb
Review: Units 9 and 10 pages 134–135		■ Understanding conversations		

Reference	pages 136–143
Grammar charts	pages 136–139
Useful lists	pages 140–142
Map of North America	page 143
Self-study audio script	pages 144–152

READING	WRITING	LIFE SKILLS	PRONUNCIATION
■ Reading a paragraph about a person's schedule ■ Reading someone's daily schedule	■ Completing a schedule ■ Completing sentences about a schedule	■ Reading an invitation	■ Pronouncing key vocabulary ■ Pronouncing times
			■ Pronouncing *a* as in *at* and *o* as in *on*
■ Reading an email about a shopping trip	■ Completing a shopping list	■ Reading a store receipt	■ Pronouncing key vocabulary ■ Pronouncing prices
■ Reading an article about the employee of the month ■ Reading a letter about people's jobs	■ Completing sentences about people's jobs	■ Reading help-wanted ads	■ Pronouncing key vocabulary
			■ Pronouncing *e* as in *red*, *i* as in *six*, and *u* as in *bus*
■ Reading an email about problems with family chores ■ Reading a chart of family chores	■ Completing a chart about family chores ■ Completing sentences about family chores	■ Reading a work order	■ Pronouncing key vocabulary
■ Reading an email to a friend	■ Completing sentences about free-time activities	■ Reading a course description	■ Pronouncing key vocabulary
			■ Reviewing pronunciation of *a*, *e*, *i*, *o*, and *u* in key vocabulary

TO THE TEACHER

What is *Ventures*?

Ventures is a six-level, four-skills, standards-based, integrated-skills series that empowers students to achieve their academic and career goals.

- Aligned to the new NRS descriptors while covering key English Language Proficiency Standards and WIOA requirements.
- A wealth of resources provide instructors with the tools for any teaching situation, making *Ventures* the most complete program.
- Promotes 21st century learning complemented by a suite of technology tools.

How Does the Third Edition Meet Today's Adult Education Needs?

- The third edition is aligned to the NRS' interpretive, productive, and interactive outcomes at each level.
- To help students develop the skills they need to succeed in college and the workplace, *Ventures* 3rd Edition offers a dedicated College and Career Readiness Section (CCRS) with 10 worksheets at each level, from Level 1 to Transitions (pages 136–155).
- Audio tracks and grammar presentations linked to QR codes can be accessed using smartphones (see page x), promoting mobile learning.
- Problem-solving activities added to each unit cover critical thinking and soft skills key to workplace readiness.
- A QR code that connects learners to an animated grammar presentation has been added, providing an additional modality especially helpful for Basic level learners.

What are the *Ventures* components?

Student's Book

Each of the core **Student's Books** contains ten topic-focused units, with five review units. The main units feature six skill-focused lessons.

- **Self-contained lessons** are perfectly paced for one-hour classes. For classes longer than 1 hour, additional resources are available via the Workbook and Online Teacher's Resources.
- **Review units** recycle and reinforce the listening, vocabulary, and grammar skills developed in the two prior units and include a pronunciation activity.

Teacher's Edition

The interleaved **Teacher's Edition** includes easy-to-follow lesson plans for every unit.

- Teaching tips address common problem areas for students and additional suggestions for expansion activities and building community.
- Additional practice material across all *Ventures* components is clearly organized in the *More Ventures* chart at the end of each lesson.
- Multiple opportunities for assessment such as unit, mid-term, and final tests are available in the Teacher's Edition. Customizable tests and test audio are available online (www.cambridge.org/ventures/resources/).

Online Teacher's Resources
www.cambridge.org/ventures/resources/

Ventures Online Teacher's Resources offer hundreds of additional worksheets and classroom materials including:

- A *placement test* that helps accurately identify the appropriate level of *Ventures* for each student.
- *Collaborative Worksheets* for each lesson develop cooperative learning and community building within the classroom.
- *Writing Worksheets* that help literacy-level students recognize shapes and write letters and numbers, while alphabet and number cards promote partner and group work.
- *Picture dictionary cards and Worksheets* that reinforce vocabulary learned in Levels Basic, 1, and 2.
- *Self-assessments* give students an opportunity to reflect on their learning. They support learner persistence and help determine whether students are ready for the unit test.

Workbook

The **Workbook** provides two pages of activities for each lesson in the Student's Book.

- If used in class, the Workbook can extend classroom instructional time by 30 minutes per lesson.
- The exercises are designed so learners can complete them in class or independently. Students can check their answers with the answer key in the back of the Workbook. Workbook exercises can be assigned in class, for homework, or as student support when a class is missed.
- Grammar charts at the back of the Workbook allow students to use the Workbook for self-study.

Literacy Workbook

The Literacy Workbook develops reading and writing readiness skills by focusing on letter formation, the conventions of writing in English, and the connection between written and spoken language. For each lesson in the Basic Student's Book, the Literacy Workbook has two pages of activities focusing on key words and sentences.

- The left-hand page is for students who are pre-, non-, or semiliterate in their own languages. Capital letters are introduced before lower case letters, and letters are sequenced based on strokes to form them; for example, straight lines such as *t* before curved lines such as *s*. Letters are presented in the context of words practiced in the lesson of the Student's Book that the workbook lesson supports.

- The right-hand page is for students who are literate in their first languages, but unfamiliar with the Roman alphabet used in English. When appropriate, students who complete the left-hand page with confidence can move to the right-hand page.

- Students who begin with the right-hand page, but require remediation, can move to the left-hand page.

Online Workbooks

The self-grading **Online Workbooks** offer programs the flexibility of introducing blended learning.

- In addition to the same high-quality practice opportunities in the print workbooks, the online workbooks provide students instant feedback.

- Teachers and programs can track student progress and time on task.

Presentation Plus
www.esource.cambridge.org

Presentation Plus allows teachers to project the contents of the Student's Book in front of the class for a livelier, interactive classroom. It is a complete solution for teachers because it includes the Class audio, answer keys, and the *Ventures* Arcade. Contact your Cambridge ESL Specialist (www.cambridge.org/cambridgeenglish/contact) to find out how to access it.

Ventures Arcade
www.cambridge.org/venturesarcade/

The Arcade is a free website where students can find additional practice for the listening, vocabulary, grammar, and reading found in the Student's Books. There is also a Citizenship section that includes questions on civics, history, government, and the N-400 application.

Unit organization

LESSON A Listening focuses students on the unit topic. The initial exercise, **Before you listen**, creates student interest with visuals that help the teacher assess what learners already know and serves as a prompt for the unit's key vocabulary. Next is **Listen**, which is based on conversations. Students relate vocabulary to meaning and relate the spoken and written forms of new theme-related vocabulary. **After you listen** concludes the lesson by practicing language related to the theme in a communicative activity, either orally with a partner or individually in a writing activity.

LESSON B focuses on vocabulary in the Basic Student's Book. It introduces vocabulary through illustrations and listening, followed by practice exercises that check understanding, relate spoken to written form, and provide conversation practice. The lesson ends with an interaction activity.

LESSON C focuses on grammar. The lessons move from a **Grammar focus** that presents the grammar point in chart form; to **Practice** exercises that check comprehension of the grammar point and provide guided practice; and, finally, to **Communicate** exercises that guide learners as they generate original answers and conversations. These lessons often include a *Culture note*, which provides information directly related to the conversation practice (such as the use of titles with last names) or a *Useful language* note, which introduces useful expressions.

LESSON D Reading develops reading skills and expands vocabulary. The lesson opens with a **Before you read** exercise, designed to activate prior knowledge and encourage learners to make predictions. The **Read** section includes audio, which provides additional practice in connecting sound with print, a skill especially important for Basic level learners. The reading section of the lesson concludes with **After you read** exercises that check comprehension. In Levels Basic, 1, and 2, the vocabulary expansion portion of the lesson is a **Picture dictionary**. It includes a *word bank*, pictures to identify, and a conversation for practicing the new words. The words expand vocabulary related to the unit topic. In Books 3 and 4, the vocabulary expansion portion of the lesson uses new vocabulary from the reading to build skills such as recognizing word families, selecting definitions based on the context of the reading, and using clues in the reading to guess meaning.

LESSON E Writing focuses on basic writing skills. In preparation for the writing, students fill in missing letters in words or missing words in sentences. Next, they fill in missing words in a paragraph, which serves as a model for them to write their information or ideas. The lesson ends with students sharing their writing with a partner.

LESSON F Another view brings the unit together with opportunities to review lesson content. **Life-skills reading** develops the scanning and skimming skills used with documents such as forms, charts, schedules, announcements, and ads. Multiple-choice questions (modeled on CASAS[1] and BEST[2]) develop test-taking skills. **Solve the problem** focuses on critical thinking, soft-skills, and workplace development. **Fun with vocabulary** provides interactive activities that review and expand the vocabulary of the unit.

---

[1] The Comprehensive Adult Student Assessment System. For more information, see www.casas.org.
[2] The Basic English Skills Test. For more information, see www.cal.org/BEST.

UNIT TOUR

The Most Complete Course for Student Success

- Helps students develop the skills needed to be college and career ready and function successfully in their community
- Covers key NRS and WIOA requirements
- Aligned with the English Language Proficiency (ELP) Standards

The Big Picture

- Introduces the unit topic and creates an opportunity for classroom discussion.
- Activates students' prior knowledge and previews the unit vocabulary.

Unit Goals

Introduces the competencies students will learn.

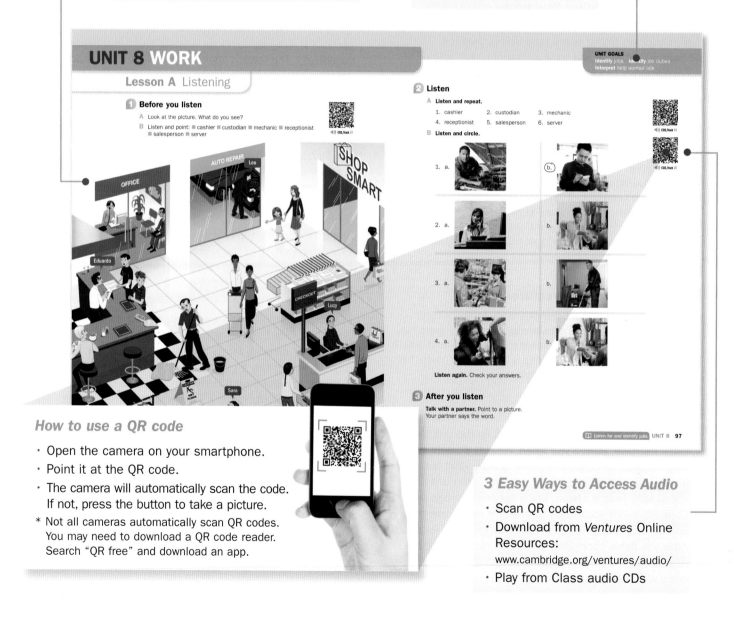

How to use a QR code

- Open the camera on your smartphone.
- Point it at the QR code.
- The camera will automatically scan the code. If not, press the button to take a picture.

* Not all cameras automatically scan QR codes. You may need to download a QR code reader. Search "QR free" and download an app.

3 Easy Ways to Access Audio

- Scan QR codes
- Download from *Ventures* Online Resources:
  www.cambridge.org/ventures/audio/
- Play from Class audio CDs

Vocabulary Practice

Explicit vocabulary practice with accompanying audio equips students with the tools necessary to succeed outside the classroom.

Additional Grammar Activities

Ensures students have the chance to practice more grammar to meet the rigor of CCRS.

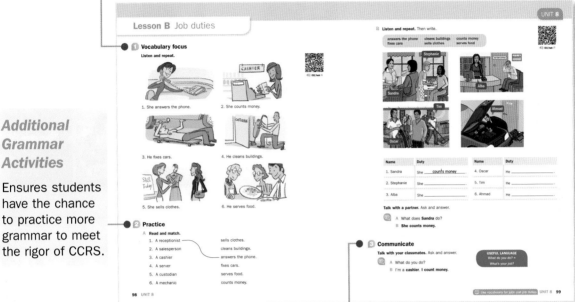

Natural Progression

Moves from controlled to communicative activities for students to ask and answer questions about familiar text, topics, and experiences.

Real-life Practice

Engages students and provides meaningful application of the grammar.

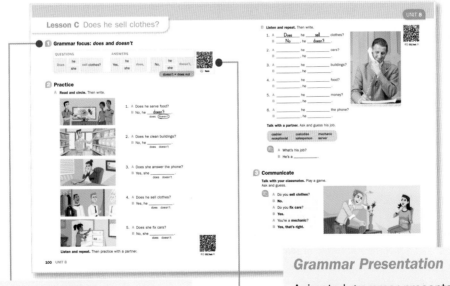

Grammar Chart

· Presents and practices the grammar point.
· Extra grammar charts online can be used for reference and give additional support.

Grammar Presentation

Animated grammar presentations to watch on mobile devices using QR codes allow for self-directed learning and develop digital literacy.

Reading

- Uses a 3-step reading approach to highlight the skills and strategies students need to succeed.
- Combines reading with writing and listening practice for an integrated approach to ensure better comprehension.
- Brings text complexity into the classroom to help students read independently and proficiently.

Picture dictionary

Expands unit vocabulary and practices pronunciation for deeper understanding of the topic.

Speaking Practice

Helps students internalize the vocabulary and relate it to their lives.

Writing

- Helps students develop a robust process-writing approach.
- Supports students to meet the challenges of work and the classroom through academic and purposeful writing practice.

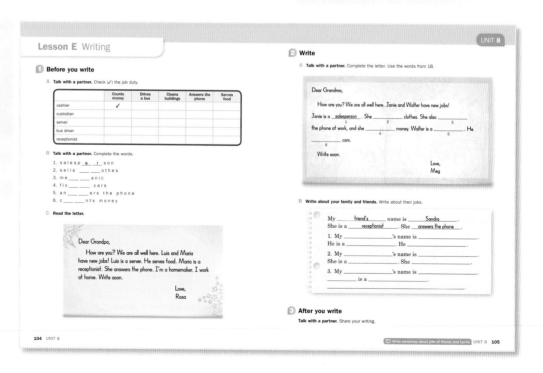

Document Literacy

Builds real-life skills through explicit practice using authentic document types.

Fun with Vocabulary

Provides interactive activities that review and expand the vocabulary of the unit.

Test-taking Skills

Prepares students for standarized tests like the BEST by familiarizing them with bubble answer format.

Problem-solving Activity

Covers critical thinking and soft skills – crucial for workplace readiness – and helps students meet WIOA requirements.

Review Pages

Provides review and confirms retention of vocabulary and grammar after every two units.

Pronunciation Activities

Gives additional opportunities to practice pronunciation and promotes spoken fluency.

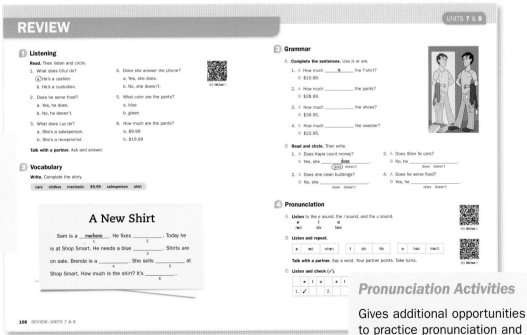

CORRELATIONS

UNIT	CASAS Competencies	Florida Adult ESOL Low Beginning	LAUSD ESL Beginning Low Competencies
Welcome Unit Pages 2–5			
Unit 1 Personal information Pages 6–17	0.1.2, 0.1.4, 0.1.5, 0.2.1, 2.3.2, 4.8.1, 6.0.1, 7.4.1, 7.4.2, 7.4.3, 7.5.1	1.01.01, 1.01.02, 1.01.03, 1.01.04, 1.01.05, 1.01.06, 1.01.10, 1.03.12, 1.04.01	I. 1a, 1b, 1c, 2, 3, 4 II. 5m III. 8, 9
Unit 2 At school Pages 18–29	0.1.2, 0.1.5, 1.4.1, 2.3.2, 4.5.1, 4.8.1, 7.4.1, 7.4.2, 7.4.3, 7.5.1	1.01.02, 1.01.04, 1.01.05, 1.03.10, 1.03.12, 1.03.16, 1.04.09	I. 3 II. 6b III. 8, 9, 11
Unit 3 Friends and family Pages 32–43	0.1.2, 0.1.4, 0.1.5, 0.2.1, 4.8.1, 7.4.1, 7.4.2, 7.4.3, 7.5.1, 8.3.1	1.01.03, 1.02.07, 1.03.12, 1.04.04, 1.05.01	I. 1d, 3 III. 9
Unit 4 Health Pages 44–55	0.1.2, 0.1.4, 0.1.5, 0.2.1, 3.1.1, 3.1.3, 3.3.1, 3.3.2, 3.4.1, 4.8.1, 7.4.1, 7.4.2, 7.4.3, 7.5.1, 8.3.2	1.01.04, 1.02.07, 1.03.12, 1.03.16, 1.05.01, 1.05.02, 1.05.03, 1.05.04, 1.07.03	I. 3 II. 7 III. 9
Unit 5 Around town Pages 58–69	0.1.2, 0.1.4, 0.1.5, 0.2.1, 1.1.3, 2.2.1, 2.2.3, 2.2.5, 2.5.4, 4.8.1, 7.1.1, 7.4.1, 7.4.2, 7.4.3, 7.4.8, 7.5.1, 7.5.6	1.01.03, 1.02.01, 1.02.02, 1.02.10, 1.03.12, 1.04.09, 1.06.01, 1.06.02, 1.06.03	I. 3 II. 5k III. 10

For more details and correlations to other state standards, go to: www.cambridge.org/ventures/correlations

Interpretive
- Identify key words and phrases relating to personal information.
- Recognize vocabulary relating to personal information and to countries and months of the year.
- Scan for key information in a reading about a new student.
- Scan for key information in an ID card.

Productive
- Use *possessive adjectives*.
- Ask and answer questions about personal information.
- Complete an ID card by giving personal information.

Interactive
- Participate in a short conversation and written exchanges about personal information.
- Project: Participate in a research project about contact information for your classmates.

Interpretive
- Identify key words and phrases relating to the classroom.
- Recognize vocabulary relating to classroom furniture, classroom objects, and days of the week.
- Scan for key information in a reading about class information and school supplies.
- Scan for key information in a class schedule.

Productive
- Use *prepositions of location*.
- Ask what someone needs and about the location of things.
- Complete sentences about class information.

Interactive
- Participate in a short conversation and written exchanges about the classroom.
- Project: Participate in a research project about shopping for school supplies.

Interpretive
- Identify key words and phrases relating to friends and family.
- Recognize vocabulary relating to family relationships, family members, and people.
- Scan for key information in a reading about family.
- Scan for key information in a housing application.

Productive
- Use *Yes/No* questions with *have*.
- Ask and answer questions about family relationships.
- Complete sentences about your family.

Interactive
- Participate in a short conversation and written exchanges about friends and family.
- Project: Participate in a research project about making a family chart.

Interpretive
- Identify key words and phrases relating to health.
- Recognize vocabulary relating to the doctor's office, health problems, and body parts.
- Scan for key information in a reading about a visit to the doctor's office.
- Scan for key information in a label on a box of medicine.

Productive
- Use *singular* and *plural nouns*.
- Ask and answer questions about health problems.
- Complete a sign-in sheet at the doctor's office.

Interactive
- Participate in a short conversation and written exchanges about health.
- Project: Participate in a research project about finding a health clinic near your home.

Interpretive
- Identify key words and phrases relating to places and locations.
- Recognize vocabulary relating to buildings, places, and transportation.
- Scan for key information in readings about a notice for a library opening and a description of someone's street.
- Scan for key information in a map.

Productive
- Use *prepositions of location* and *where* questions.
- Ask and answer questions about the location of buildings and places.
- Complete sentences describing your street.

Interactive
- Participate in a short conversation and written exchanges about places and locations.
- Project: Participate in a research project about creating a map of your community.

UNIT	CASAS Competencies	Florida Adult ESOL Low Beginning	LAUSD ESL Beginning Low Competencies
Unit 6 Time Pages 70–81	0.1.2, 0.1.4, 0.1.5, 0.2.1, 2.3.1, 2.3.2, 4.5.3, 4.8.1, 6.0.1, 7.1.1, 7.1.4, 7.4.1, 7.4.2, 7.4.3, 7.5.1	1.01.03, 1.01.05, 1.02.02, 1.03.09, 1.03.12, 1.03.16, 1.04.01	I. 3 II. 6a, 6c
Unit 7 Shopping Pages 84–95	0.1.2, 0.1.4, 0.1.5, 0.2.1, 1.1.6, 1.2.1, 1.2.2, 1.3.9, 1.6.3, 4.8.1, 6.0.1, 7.1.1, 7.4.1, 7.4.2, 7.4.3, 7.5.1, 8.1.4	1.01.03, 1.03.12, 1.03.16, 1.04.01, 1.04.02, 1.04.06	I. 3 III. 13, 14
Unit 8 Work Pages 96–107	0.1.2, 0.1.4, 0.1.5, 0.2.1, 1.1.6, 2.3.2, 4.1.3, 4.1.6, 4.1.8, 4.8.1, 4.8.2, 6.0.1, 7.1.1, 7.1.4, 7.4.1, 7.4.2, 7.5.1	1.01.03, 1.03.01, 1.03.02, 1.03.12, 1.03.14	I. 3 III. 8, 13
Unit 9 Daily living Pages 110–121	0.1.2, 0.1.5, 0.2.1, 0.2.4, 1.4.1, 1.7.4, 4.1.8, 4.7.3, 4.7.4, 4.8.1, 7.1.1, 7.4.1, 7.4.2, 7.4.3, 7.5.6, 8.1.4, 8.2.1, 8.2.2, 8.2.3, 8.2.4, 8.2.5	1.01.03, 1.01.04, 1.03.12	I. 3 II. 7 III. 8
Unit 10 Free time Pages 122–133	0.1.1, 0.1.2, 0.1.4, 0.1.5, 0.2.1, 0.2.4, 2.3.1, 2.3.2, 4.8.1, 7.1.1, 7.4.1, 7.4.2, 7.4.3, 7.5.1, 7.5.6	1.01.02, 1.01.03, 1.01.04, 1.03.12	I. 3 II. 5

For more details and correlations to other state standards, go to: www.cambridge.org/ventures/correlations

NRS Educational Functioning Level Descriptors

Interpretive
- Identify key words and phrases relating to daily activities and time.
- Recognize vocabulary relating to clock time, activities, and events and times of the day.
- Scan for key information in someone's schedule.
- Scan for key information in an invitation.

Productive
- Use *Yes/No* questions with *be*.
- Ask and answer questions about the time and about events.
- Complete a schedule.

Interactive
- Participate in a short conversation and written exchanges about daily activities and time.
- Project: Participate in a research project using the Internet to find library hours.

Interpretive
- Identify key words and phrases relating to clothes and prices.
- Recognize vocabulary relating to clothing, prices, and colors.
- Scan for key information in an e-mail about a shopping trip.
- Scan for key information in a store receipt.

Productive
- Use *how much is* and *how much are* questions.
- Ask and answer questions about prices and identify colors of clothing.
- Complete a shopping list.

Interactive
- Participate in a short conversation and written exchanges about clothes and prices.
- Project: Participate in a research project using the Internet to find a shopping center near your home.

Interpretive
- Identify key words and phrases relating to jobs and skills.
- Recognize vocabulary relating to names of jobs and job duties.
- Scan for key information in a reading about people's jobs and the employee of the month.
- Scan for key information in help-wanted ads.

Productive
- Use *Yes/No* questions with *simple present* and short answers with *does/doesn't*.
- Ask and answer questions about jobs and job duties.
- Complete sentences about people's jobs.

Interactive
- Participate in a short conversation and written exchanges about jobs and skills.
- Project: Participate in a research project about finding a job.

Interpretive
- Identify key words and phrases relating to home responsibilities.
- Recognize vocabulary relating to chores and rooms of a house.
- Scan for key information in an e-mail and a chart about family chores.
- Scan for key information in a work order

Productive
- Use *what* questions with the *present continuous*.
- Ask and answer questions about family chores and people's activities.
- Complete a chart about family chores.

Interactive
- Participate in a short conversation and written exchanges about home responsibilities.
- Project: Participate in a research project about creating and giving a class survey.

Interpretive
- Identify key words and phrases relating to free-time activities.
- Recognize vocabulary relating to free-time activities.
- Scan for key information in an e-mail to a friend.
- Scan for key information in a course description.

Productive
- Use *like to + verb* and *what* questions with *like to + verb*.
- Ask and answer questions about free-time activities.
- Complete sentences about free-time activities.

Interactive
- Participate in a short conversation and written exchanges about free-time activities.
- Project: Participate in a research project about a movie theater near your home.

(Top row) Dennis Johnson, K. Lynn Savage; (bottom row) Gretchen Bitterlin, Donna Price, and Sylvia G. Ramirez. Together, the *Ventures* author team has more than 200 years teaching ESL as well as other roles that support adult immigrants and refugees, from teacher's aide to dean.

Gretchen Bitterlin has taught Citizenship, ESL, and family literacy through the San Diego Community College District and served as coordinator of the non-credit Continuing Education ESL program. She was an item writer for CASAS tests and chaired the task force that developed the TESOL Adult Education Program Standards. She is recipient of The President's Distinguished Leadership Award from her district and co-author of *English for Adult Competency*. Gretchen holds an MA in TESOL from the University of Arizona.

Dennis Johnson had his first language-teaching experience as a Peace Corps volunteer in South Korea. Following that teaching experience, he became an in-country ESL trainer. After returning to the United States, he began teaching credit and non-credit ESL at City College of San Francisco. As ESL site coordinator, he has provided guidance to faculty in selecting textbooks. He is the author of *Get Up and Go* and co-author of *The Immigrant Experience*. Dennis is the demonstration teacher on the *Ventures Professional Development DVD*. Dennis holds an MA in music from Stanford University.

Donna Price began her ESL career teaching EFL in Madagascar. She is currently associate professor of ESL and vocational ESL / technology resource instructor for the Continuing Education Program, San Diego Community College District. She has served as an author and a trainer for CALPRO, the California Adult Literacy Professional Development Project, co-authoring training modules on contextualizing and integrating workforce skills into the ESL classroom. She is a recipient of the TESOL Newbury House Award for Excellence in Teaching, and she is author of *Skills for Success*. Donna holds an MA in linguistics from San Diego State University.

Sylvia G. Ramirez is a Professor Emeritus at MiraCosta College, a teacher educator, writer, consultant, and a recipient of the California Hayward award for excellence in education, honoring her teaching and professional activities. She is an online instructor for the TESOL Core Certificate. Her MA is in education / counseling from Point Loma University, and she has certificates in ESOL and in online teaching.

K. Lynn Savage first taught English in Japan. She began teaching ESL at City College of San Francisco in 1974, where she has taught all levels of non-credit ESL and has served as Vocational ESL Resource Teacher. She has trained teachers for adult education programs around the country as well as abroad. She chaired the committee that developed *ESL Model Standards for Adult Education Programs* (California, 1992) and is the author, co-author, and editor of many ESL materials including *Crossroads Café*, *Teacher Training through Video*, *Parenting for Academic Success*, *Building Life Skills*, *Picture Stories*, *May I Help You?*, and *English That Works*. Lynn holds an MA in TESOL from Teachers College, Columbia University.

TO THE STUDENT

Welcome to *Ventures* Basic!

Enjoy your book in class.

Enjoy your book at home.

Listen to the audio on your smartphone.
Look for the picture in your book.
Review and practice at home.

Good luck!

The Author Team
Gretchen Bitterlin
Dennis Johnson
Donna Price
Sylvia Ramirez
K. Lynn Savage

WELCOME

1 Meet your classmates

Look at the picture. What do you see?

2 The alphabet

A **Listen and point.** Look at the alphabet.

CD1, Track 02

Aa	Bb	Cc	Dd	Ee	Ff	Gg	Hh	I i
Jj	Kk	Ll	Mm	Nn	Oo	Pp	Qq	Rr
Ss	Tt	Uu	Vv	Ww	Xx	Yy	Zz	

Listen again and repeat.

B **Listen and write.**

CD1, Track 03

1. __A__ nita   2. _____ aniel   3. _____ eizhi   4. _____ uri

5. _____ ranco   6. _____ ee   7. _____ akim   8. _____ arla

C **Write your name.**

_____

Talk with 3 classmates. Say your name. Spell your name.

Hello. I'm Anita.
That's A-N-I-T-A.

3 Classroom directions

A Listen and point. Look at the pictures.

1. Look.

2. Listen.

3. Point.

4. Repeat.

5. Talk.

6. Write.

7. Read.

8. Circle.

9. Match.

Listen again and repeat.

B Talk with a partner. Say a word.
Your partner points to the picture.

Look.

4 Numbers

A **Listen and point.** Look at the numbers.

CD1, Track 05

1 one	2 two	3 three	4 four	5 five
6 six	7 seven	8 eight	9 nine	10 ten
11 eleven	12 twelve	13 thirteen	14 fourteen	15 fifteen
16 sixteen	17 seventeen	18 eighteen	19 nineteen	20 twenty

Listen again and repeat.

B **Listen and write the number.**

1. ___6___   2. _____   3. _____   4. _____
5. _____   6. _____   7. _____   8. _____

CD 1, Track 06

Talk with a partner. Check your answers.

Lesson A Listening

1 Before you listen

A Look at the picture. What do you see?

B Listen and point: ■ area code ■ country ■ first name ■ ID card
■ last name ■ phone number

CD1, Track 07

UNIT GOALS
Recognize names and vocabulary for personal identification
Identify countries of origin   Complete an ID card

2 Listen

A   Listen and repeat.

1. area code   2. country   3. first name

4. ID card   5. last name   6. phone number

🔊 CD1, Track 08

🔊 CD1, Track 09

B   Listen and circle.

1. a.    b.

2. a.    b.

USEFUL LANGUAGE
Say *oh* for *zero*.

2	0	1
two	oh	one

3. a.    b.

4. a. 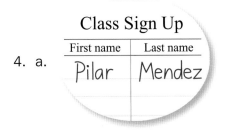   b.

Listen again. Check your answers.

3 After you listen

Talk with a partner. Point to a picture.
Your partner says the words.

Lesson B Countries

1 Vocabulary focus

Listen and repeat.

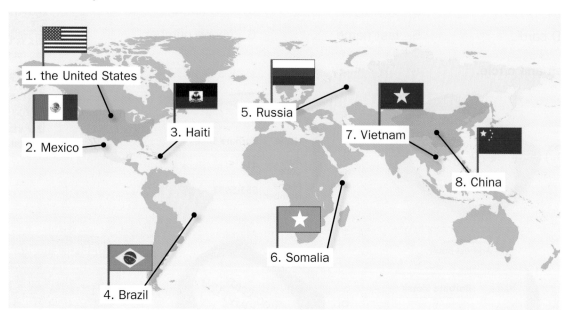

1. the United States
2. Mexico
3. Haiti
4. Brazil
5. Russia
6. Somalia
7. Vietnam
8. China

2 Practice

A Read and match.

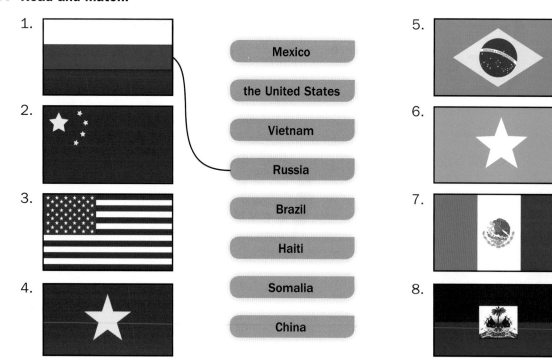

Mexico

the United States

Vietnam

Russia

Brazil

Haiti

Somalia

China

B **Listen and repeat.** Then write.

CD1, Track 11

Name	Country	Name	Country
1. Ivan	Russia	4. Elsa	
2. Asad		5. Luisa	
3. Eduardo		6. Jun-Ming	

Talk with a partner. Ask and answer.

A Where is **Ivan** from?

B **Russia.**

3 Communicate

Talk in a group. Ask and answer. Complete the chart.

A What's your name?

B **Binh.**

A Where are you from?

B **Vietnam.**

Name	Country
Binh	Vietnam

Lesson C What's your name?

1 Grammar focus: *my, your, his, her*

QUESTIONS			ANSWERS		
	your		My		Angela.
What's	his	name?	His	name is	Kevin.
	her		Her		Julia.

What's = What is

Watch

2 Practice

A **Read and circle.** Then write.

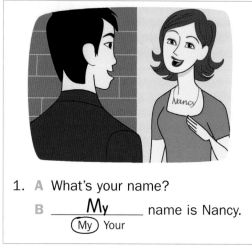

1. A What's your name?
    B _____**My**_____ name is Nancy.
       (My) Your

2. A What's his name?
    B _____ name is Chin.
       His   Her

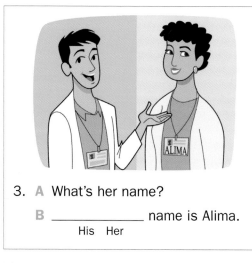

3. A What's her name?
    B _____ name is Alima.
       His   Her

4. A What's your name?
    B _____ name is Vincent.
       My   Your

Listen and repeat. Then practice with a partner.

CD1, Track 12

10 UNIT 1

B **Listen and repeat.** Then write.

🔊 CD1, Track 13

TOPS ADULT SCHOOL

First name: Jack
Last name: Lee
Area code: 203
Phone number: 555-9687

TOPS ADULT SCHOOL

First name: Sara
Last name: Garza
Area code: 415
Phone number: 555-3702

What's his . . . ?		What's her . . . ?	
1. first __name__	Jack	5. _____ code	415
2. last _____	Lee	6. _____ number	555-3702
3. area _____	203	7. _____ name	Garza
4. phone _____	555-9687	8. _____ name	Sara

Talk with a partner. Ask and answer.

A What's **his first name**?

B **Jack.**

③ Communicate

Talk with your classmates. Complete the chart.

A What's your **first name**?

B My **first name** is **Yuri**.

> **USEFUL LANGUAGE**
> *How do you spell Yuri?*
> *Y-U-R-I*

First name	Last name	Area code	Phone number
Yuri			

Lesson D Reading

METRO ADULT SCHOOL

1 Before you read

Talk about the picture.
What do you see?

2 Read

Listen and read.

CD1, Track 14

> # Welcome!
>
> Meet our new student.
>
> His first name is Ernesto.
>
> His last name is Delgado.
>
> He is from Mexico.
>
> Welcome, Ernesto Delgado!

3 After you read

Read the sentences. Circle *Yes* or *No*.

1. His name is Ernesto Mexico.	Yes	(No)
2. His first name is Ernesto.	Yes	No
3. His last name is Delgado.	Yes	No
4. He is from Ecuador.	Yes	No

4 Picture dictionary Months of the year

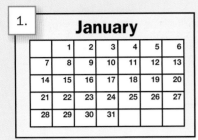

1.	January					
		1	2	3	4	5	6
7	8	9	10	11	12	13
14	15	16	17	18	19	20
21	22	23	24	25	26	27
28	29	30	31			

2.	February					
				1	2	3
4	5	6	7	8	9	10
11	12	13	14	15	16	17
18	19	20	21	22	23	24
25	26	27	28			

3.	March					
				1	2	3
4	5	6	7	8	9	10
11	12	13	14	15	16	17
18	19	20	21	22	23	24
25	26	27	28	29	30	31

4.	April					
1	2	3	4	5	6	7
8	9	10	11	12	13	14
15	16	17	18	19	20	21
22	23	24	25	26	27	28
29	30					

5.	May					
		1	2	3	4	5
6	7	8	9	10	11	12
13	14	15	16	17	18	19
20	21	22	23	24	25	26
27	28	29	30	31		

6.	June					
					1	2
3	4	5	6	7	8	9
10	11	12	13	14	15	16
17	18	19	20	21	22	23
24	25	26	27	28	29	30

7.	July					
1	2	3	4	5	6	7
8	9	10	11	12	13	14
15	16	17	18	19	20	21
22	23	24	25	26	27	28
29	30	31				

8.	August					
			1	2	3	4
5	6	7	8	9	10	11
12	13	14	15	16	17	18
19	20	21	22	23	24	25
26	27	28	29	30	31	

9.	September					
						1
2	3	4	5	6	7	8
9	10	11	12	13	14	15
16	17	18	19	20	21	22
23 30	24	25	26	27	28	29

10.	October					
		1	2	3	4	5	6
7	8	9	10	11	12	13
14	15	16	17	18	19	20
21	22	23	24	25	26	27
28	29	30	31			

11.	November					
				1	2	3
4	5	6	7	8	9	10
11	12	13	14	15	16	17
18	19	20	21	22	23	24
25	26	27	28	29	30	

12.	December					
						1
2	3	4	5	6	7	8
9	10	11	12	13	14	15
16	17	18	19	20	21	22
23 30	24 31	25	26	27	28	29

A **Listen and repeat.** Look at the Picture dictionary.

B **Talk with your classmates.** Complete the chart.

CD1, Track 15

  A What's your name?

  B **Eva.**

  A When's your birthday?

  B **In April.**

Name	Month
Eva	April

Lesson E Writing

1 Before you write

A **Talk with a partner.** Complete the words.

1. <u>f</u> i r s t
2. ____ a s t
3. ____ a m e
4. a r e a ____ o d e
5. p h o n e ____ u m b e r

B **Read the ID card.** Complete the sentences.

Central Adult School Library

Wong
Last name

Linda
First name

916
Area code

555-7834
Phone number

China
Country

Linda Wong
Signature

CULTURE NOTE
Your signature is how
you write your name.

1. Her _____ _____ is Linda.
2. Her _____ _____ is Wong.
3. Her _____ _____ is 916.
4. Her _____ _____ is 555-7834.
5. She is from _____ .

2 Write

A **Complete the ID card.** Write about yourself.

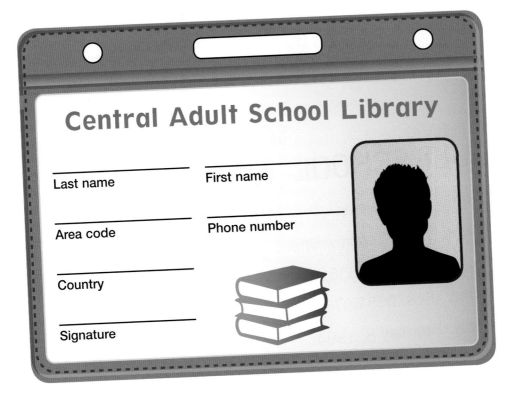

Central Adult School Library

_____
Last name

_____
First name

_____
Area code

_____
Phone number

_____
Country

_____
Signature

B **Complete the sentences.** Write about yourself.

1. My first name is _____.
2. My last name is _____.
3. My area code is _____.
4. My phone number is _____.
5. My birthday is in _____.

3 After you write

Talk with a partner. Share your writing.

1 Life-skills reading

MIDTOWN ADULT SCHOOL

Name: Samir Ahmed

Address: 1432 Woodrow Street
Tampa, FL 33612

Phone: (813) 555-6978

Birthday: February 8, 1994

Samir Ahmed
SIGNATURE

A Read the sentences. Look at the ID card. Fill in the answer.

1. His first name is _____.

   (A) Ahmed

   (B) Woodrow

   (●) Samir

2. His area code is _____.

   (A) 33612

   (B) 813

   (C) 555

3. His birthday is in _____.

   (A) January

   (B) February

   (C) August

4. His last name is _____.

   (A) Ahmed

   (B) Woodrow

   (C) Tampa

B Solve the problem. Which solution is best? Circle your opinion.

Samir's ID card is wrong. His address is 1342 Woodrow Street. What should he do?

1. Write 1342 on the ID card.

2. Tell the teacher.

3. Other: _____

2 Fun with vocabulary

A What word is different? Circle the word.

1. **Countries**

   Mexico   China   (November)   Somalia

2. **Months**

   April   September   May   Russia

3. **Phone numbers**

   555-4861   555-6978   415   555-7934

4. **Area codes**

   555-6948   813   212   915

5. **First names**

   Linda   Alima   Nasser   Mexico

6. **Last names**

   Cruz   February   Delgado   Lee

Talk with a partner. Check your answers.

B Work with a partner. Write the months in order.

April	August	December	February	January	July
June	March	May	November	October	September

1	2	3	4
January			

5	6	7	8

9	10	11	12

UNIT 2 AT SCHOOL

Lesson A Listening

1 Before you listen

A Look at the picture. What do you see?

B Listen and point: ■ a book ■ a chair ■ a computer ■ a desk
   ■ a notebook ■ a pencil

CD1, Track 16

Ventures Basic, Unit 2
Pages 18 and 19

Sue

UNIT GOALS
Identify classroom objects   **Name** location of classroom objects
Complete school information form

2 Listen

A Listen and repeat.

1. a book
2. a chair
3. a computer
4. a desk
5. a notebook
6. a pencil

◀)) CD1, Track 17

B Listen and circle.

◀)) CD1, Track 18

1. a.   b.

2. a.    b.

3. a.    b.

4. a.    b.

Listen again. Check your answers.

3 After you listen

Talk with a partner. Point to a picture.
Your partner says the words.

Lesson B Classroom objects

1 Vocabulary focus

Listen and repeat.

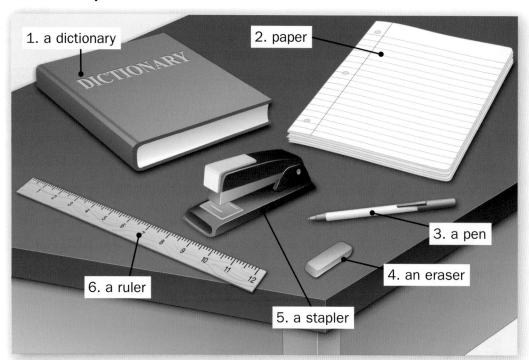

1. a dictionary
2. paper
3. a pen
4. an eraser
5. a stapler
6. a ruler

CD1, Track 19

2 Practice

A Read and match.

1.

2.

3.

paper

an eraser

a dictionary

a stapler

a ruler

a pen

4.

5.

6.

B **Listen and repeat.** Then write.

> a dictionary   an eraser   paper
> a pen   a ruler   a stapler

CD1, Track 20

1. a dictionary
2.
3.
4.
5.
6.

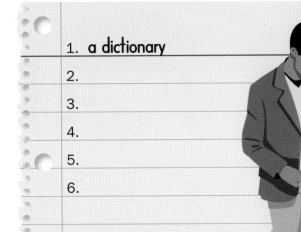

Talk with a partner. Act it out.

A What do you need, **Carla**?

B **A dictionary.**

A Here you are.

3 Communicate

Talk with your classmates. Complete the chart.

A What do you need, **Mahmoud**?

B **An eraser.**

Name	Classroom object
Mahmoud	an eraser

1. Carla
2. Daw
3. Stefan
4. Felicia
5. Kim
6. Pablo

Lesson C Where's my pencil?

1 Grammar focus: *in*, *on*, and *under*

in the desk

on the desk

under the desk

Watch

2 Practice

A **Read and circle.** Then write.

1. **A** Where's my pencil?
   B _____**In**_____ the desk.
   (In) On Under

2. **A** Where's my notebook?
   B _____ the desk.
   In On Under

3. **A** Where's my pen?
   B _____ the floor.
   In On Under

4. **A** Where's my dictionary?
   B _____ the table.
   In On Under

5. **A** Where's my ruler?
   B _____ the table.
   In On Under

6. **A** Where's my paper?
   B _____ the desk.
   In On Under

Listen and repeat. Then practice with a partner.

◀)) CD1, Track 21

B **Look at the picture.** Match the words.

1. my book — under the chair
2. my stapler — on the desk
3. my notebook — in the desk
4. my ruler — on the book

5. my paper — in the notebook
6. my pen — under the desk
7. my pencil — on the paper
8. my dictionary — on the chair

Talk with a partner. Act it out.

A Where's my **book**?
B **In the desk.**
A Thanks.

③ Communicate

Talk with a partner. Complete the chart.

A Where's my **pencil**?
B **On the desk.**

> **USEFUL LANGUAGE**
> *I don't know.*

my pencil	on the desk
my book	
my paper	
my pen	
my dictionary	
my notebook	

Lesson D Reading

1 Before you read

Talk about the picture.
What do you see?

2 Read

Listen and read.

Sue,

It's Monday, your first day of English class! You need a pencil, eraser, notebook, and dictionary. The pencil is in the desk. The eraser is on the desk. The notebook is on my computer. And the dictionary is under the chair.

Have fun at school!

Mom

CD1, Track 22

3 After you read

Read and match.

1.

The pencil is in the desk.

The notebook is on the computer.

The dictionary is under the chair.

The eraser is on the desk.

3.

2.

4.

4 **Picture dictionary** Days of the week

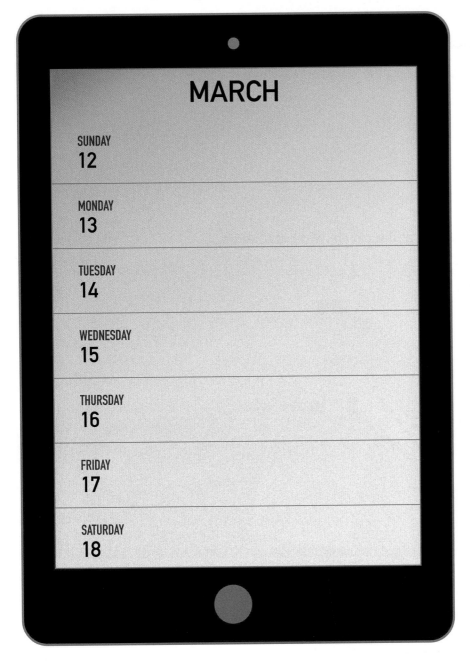

MARCH

SUNDAY	12
MONDAY	13
TUESDAY	14
WEDNESDAY	15
THURSDAY	16
FRIDAY	17
SATURDAY	18

A **Listen and repeat.** Look at the Picture dictionary.

B **Talk with a partner.** Point and ask. Your partner answers.

　A What day is it?

　B **Monday.**

◀)) CD1, Track 23

Lesson E Writing

1 **Before you write**

A **Talk with a partner.** Complete the words.

1. e r a s e __r__

2. d i c t i o n a r ____

3. p e ____

4. p e n c i ____

5. n o t e b o o ____

B **Talk with a partner.** Look at the picture. Write the words.

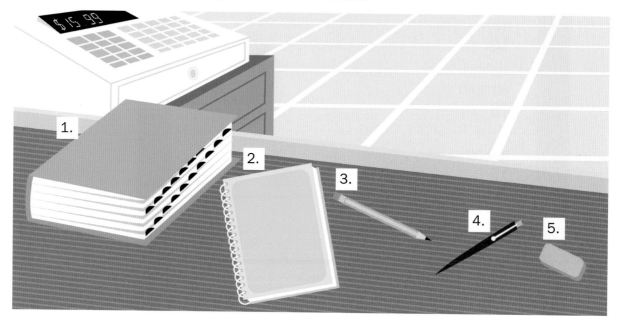

1. dictionary
2. _____
3. _____
4. _____
5. _____

2 **Write**

A **Read the memo.**

Welcome to Miami Adult School!

The first day of school is Monday.

Your teacher is Ms. Moreno.

Your class is in Room 101.

For class, you need:

a dictionary

a notebook

a pencil

a pen

an eraser

B **Complete the memo.** Write about yourself.

The first day of school is ⎯⎯⎯⎯⎯⎯⎯⎯⎯.

My teacher is ⎯⎯⎯⎯⎯⎯⎯⎯⎯.

My class is in Room ⎯⎯⎯⎯.

For class, I need ⎯⎯⎯⎯⎯⎯⎯⎯.

I need ⎯⎯⎯⎯⎯⎯⎯.

I need ⎯⎯⎯⎯⎯⎯⎯.

I need ⎯⎯⎯⎯⎯⎯⎯.

I need ⎯⎯⎯⎯⎯⎯⎯.

3 **After you write**

Talk with a partner. Share your writing.

Lesson F Another view

1 Life-skills reading

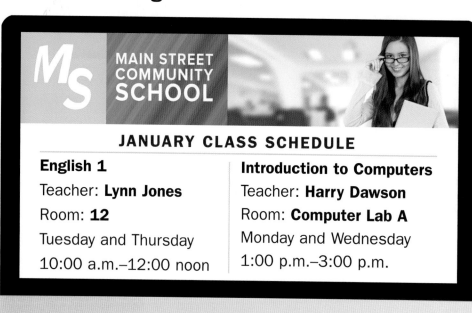

MAIN STREET COMMUNITY SCHOOL

JANUARY CLASS SCHEDULE

English 1	Introduction to Computers
Teacher: **Lynn Jones**	Teacher: **Harry Dawson**
Room: **12**	Room: **Computer Lab A**
Tuesday and Thursday	Monday and Wednesday
10:00 a.m.–12:00 noon	1:00 p.m.–3:00 p.m.

A Read the sentences. Look at the class schedule. Fill in the answer.

1. The English class is on _____.

    A Monday and Wednesday

    B Tuesday and Thursday

    C Tuesday and Wednesday

2. The computer class is on _____.

    A Monday and Wednesday

    B Tuesday and Thursday

    C Monday and Tuesday

3. The English class is in _____.

    A Room 1

    B Room 12

    C Lab A

4. The computer class is in _____.

    A Lab A

    B Lab B

    C Room 1

B Solve the problem. Which solution is best? Circle your opinion.

Marcos needs English. Main Street Community School has English classes on Tuesday and Thursday. Marcos works on Tuesday and Thursday. What should he do?

1. Take the computer class.

2. Look for another English class on Mondays and Wednesdays.

3. Other: _____

2 Fun with vocabulary

A **Talk with a partner.** What's in your classroom? Check (✔).

- ☐ a book
- ☐ a chair
- ☐ a computer
- ☐ a desk
- ☐ a dictionary
- ☐ an eraser
- ☐ a notebook
- ☐ paper
- ☐ a pen
- ☐ a pencil
- ☐ a ruler
- ☐ a stapler

B **Circle the words in the puzzle.**

| book | chair | computer | desk | dictionary | eraser |
| notebook | paper | pen | pencil | ruler | stapler |

```
h   s   h   f   e   (b   o   o   k)  t   z   a
q   u   p   e   n   c   i   l   a   f   r   s
l   i   g   o   w   n   e   r   a   s   e   r
v   y   b   d   e   s   k   a   f   l   k   o
d   i   c   t   i   o   n   a   r   y   o   j
f   e   t   h   s   t   a   p   l   e   r   e
w   r   n   n   o   t   e   b   o   o   k   r
p   e   n   k   v   l   z   o   j   s   y   n
o   t   c   o   m   p   u   t   e   r   m   q
t   r   u   l   e   r   g   a   r   x   z   a
h   o   m   t   c   z   e   c   h   a   i   r
p   a   p   e   r   n   y   i   d   e   m   t
```

REVIEW

1 Listening

Read. Then listen and circle.

1. What's his first name?

   a. Ali

   (b.) Hassan

2. What's his last name?

   a. Ali

   b. Garcia

3. Where is he from?

   a. Mexico

   b. Somalia

4. When is his birthday?

   a. in August

   b. in October

5. Where's the notebook?

   a. on the desk

   b. on the chair

6. Where's the paper?

   a. in the notebook

   b. on the chair

🔊 CD1, Track 24

Talk with a partner. Ask and answer.

2 Vocabulary

Write. Complete the story.

book   Brazil   card   February   name   Tuesday

Welcome, Luisa Pinto!

Luisa is a new student. She is from ____Brazil____ . Her
                                          1

last _____ is Pinto. Her birthday is in _____ .
          2   3

In fact, her birthday is on _____ . Happy birthday!
                                  4

Luisa needs a _____ and an ID _____ .
                    5   6

Welcome, Luisa!

30   REVIEW: UNITS 1 & 2

③ Grammar

A Complete the sentences.

Use *in*, *on*, or *under*.

1. The pen is ___under___ the notebook.

2. The dictionary is _____ the desk.

3. The book is _____ the chair.

4. The stapler is _____ the desk.

B Read and circle. Then write.

1. _____His_____ name is Alberto.
   ⓗⒾⓢ Her

2. _____ name is Layla.
   His   Her

3. A What is _____ name?
            his   your

   B _____ name is Kim.
       My   Your

④ Pronunciation

A Listen to the *a* sound and the *o* sound.

   a   **o**
n**a**me   ph**o**ne

🔊 CD1, Track 25

B Listen and repeat.

a	name	day	say

o	phone	code	note

Talk with a partner. Say a word. Your partner points. Take turns.

🔊 CD1, Track 26

C Listen and check (✓).

	a	o		a	o		a	o		a	o		a	o
1.	✓		2.			3.			4.			5.		

🔊 CD1, Track 27

UNIT 3 FRIENDS AND FAMILY

Lesson A Listening

1 Before you listen

A Look at the picture. What do you see?

B Listen and point: ■ daughter ■ father ■ grandfather ■ grandmother ■ mother ■ son

CD1, Track 28

UNIT GOALS
Identify family members **Describe** a family picture
Interpret a housing application

2 Listen

A Listen and repeat.

1. daughter   2. father   3. grandfather

4. grandmother 5. mother   6. son

CD1, Track 29

B Listen and circle.

CD1, Track 30

1. (a.)    b.

2. a.    (b.)

3. a.    (b.)

4. a.    (b.)

Listen again. Check your answers.

3 After you listen

Talk with a partner. Point to a picture and ask.
Your partner says the words.

Who's that?

The grandmother.

Lesson B Family members

1 Vocabulary focus

Listen and repeat.

◗)) CD1, Track 31

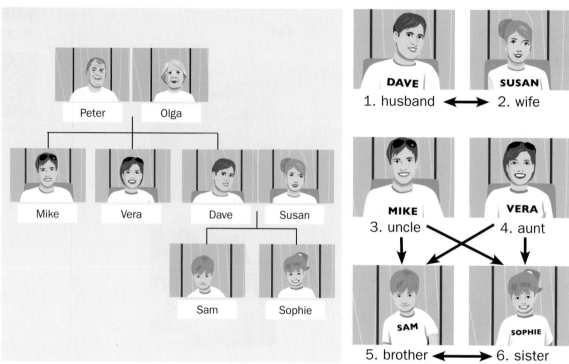

2 Practice

A Read and match.

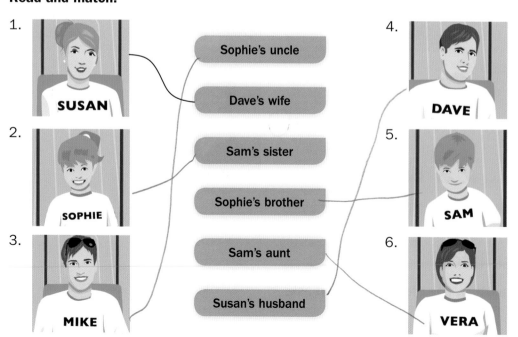

1. SUSAN
2. SOPHIE
3. MIKE

- Sophie's uncle
- Dave's wife
- Sam's sister
- Sophie's brother
- Sam's aunt
- Susan's husband

4. DAVE
5. SAM
6. VERA

B **Listen and repeat.** Then write.

aunt   brother   husband   sister   uncle   wife

◀)) CD1, Track 32

Who is . . . ?		Who is . . . ?	
1. Vera	Sam's ___aunt___	4. Susan	Dave's _wife_
2. Mike	Sam's _uncle_	5. Sam	Sophie's _Brother_
3. Sophie	Sam's _Sister_	6. Dave	Susan's _husband_

Talk with a partner. Ask and answer.

A Who is **Vera**?

B **Sam's aunt.**

3 Communicate

Complete the chart about your family. Then talk with a partner.

Name	Family member
Habib	brother

A Who is **Habib**?

B My **brother**.

1 Grammar focus: *Do you have . . . ?*

QUESTIONS	ANSWERS					
Do you have a sister?	Yes,	I / we	do.	No,	I / we	don't.

don't = do not

👁 Watch

2 Practice

A **Read and circle.** Then write.

1. A Do you have a brother?
   B ___Yes, I do.___
      (Yes, I do.) No, I don't.

2. A Do you have a sister?
   B _____
      Yes, we do.   No, we don't.

3. A Do you have a son?
   B _____
      Yes, I do.   No, I don't.

4. A Do you have a daughter?
   B _____
      Yes, we do.   No, we don't.

5. A Do you have a wife?
   B _____
      Yes, I do.   No, I don't.

Listen and repeat. Then practice with a partner.

🔊 CD1, Track 33

B **Listen and repeat.** Then write.

◀)) CD1, Track 34

Do you have a . . . ?		Do you have a . . . ?	
1. sister	**yes**	4. son	
2. brother		5. daughter	
3. husband		6. grandmother	

Talk with a partner. You are Ana. Ask and answer.

A Do you have **a sister**?

B **Yes, I do.**

A What's **her** name?

B **Diana.**

A Do you have a **brother**?

B **No, I don't.**

3 Communicate

Talk with your classmates. Complete the chart.

Do you have a . . . ?	Dinh					
	Yes	No	Yes	No	Yes	No
son		✓				
daughter	✓					
sister	✓					
brother	✓					

Lesson D Reading

1 Before you read

Talk about the picture. What do you see?

2 Read

Listen and read.

CD1, Track 35

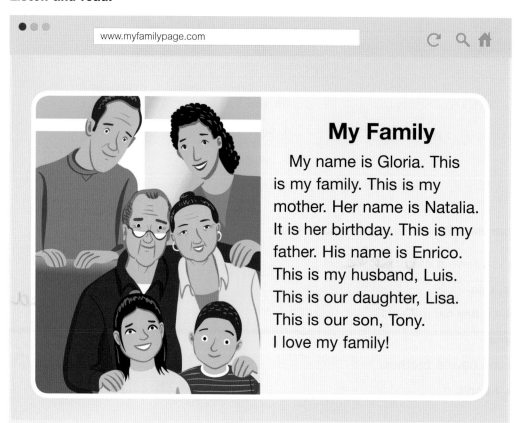

www.myfamilypage.com

My Family

My name is Gloria. This is my family. This is my mother. Her name is Natalia. It is her birthday. This is my father. His name is Enrico. This is my husband, Luis. This is our daughter, Lisa. This is our son, Tony. I love my family!

3 After you read

Read and circle. Then write.

1. Luis is Gloria's _____ husband _____.
   father (husband)

2. Natalia is Gloria's _____.
   daughter   mother

3. Tony is Gloria's _____.
   brother   son

4. Enrico is Gloria's _____.
   father   mother

5. Lisa is Gloria's _____.
   sister   daughter

4 **Picture dictionary** People

1. baby

2. girl

3. boy

4. teenager

5. woman

6. man

A **Listen and repeat.** Look at the picture dictionary.

B **Talk with a partner.** Say a word. Your partner points to the picture.

A Show me the **man**.
B Here's the **man**.

CD1, Track 36

1 Before you write

A **Talk with a partner.** Complete the words.

Frank's Family

Frank

1. __d__ a u g h t e r

2. ____ i f e

3. ____ i s t e r

4. ____ a b y

5. ____ o n

6. ____ r o t h e r

B **Talk with a partner.** Look at the picture. Complete the story.

My Wonderful Family

My name is Frank. This is my family. This is my _____*wife*_____,
1

Marie. This is our _____. His name is Patrick. This is our
2

_____. Her name is Annie. This is our new _____,
3 4

Jason. He is a boy. Patrick is his _____. Annie is his
5

_____. I have a wonderful family!
6

2 Write

A Draw a picture of your family.

B Write about your picture.

daughter   father   husband   mother   son   wife

My Wonderful Family

My name is _____. This is my family.

This is my _____. _____ name is _____.
His   Her

This is my _____. _____ name is _____.
His   Her

This is my _____. _____ name is _____.
His   Her

This is my _____. _____ name is _____.
His   Her

I love my family!

3 After you write

Talk with a partner. Share your writing.

1 Life-skills reading

KB 🏠 **PROPERTY MANAGEMENT COMPANY**
230 Central Street, Philadelphia, PA 19019 (215) 555-1863

HOUSING APPLICATION

Directions: Complete the form. Please print.

What is your name? Ali Azari

Who will live with you in the house?

NAME	RELATIONSHIP
Shohreh Azari	wife
Azam Javadi	mother
Omid Azari	son
Leila Azari	daughter
Soraya Azari	daughter

A Read the questions. Look at the housing application. Fill in the answer.

1. Who is Shohreh Azari?

   (A) Ali's daughter

   (B) Ali's wife

   (C) Ali's son

2. Who is Soraya Azari?

   (A) Ali's daughter

   (B) Ali's mother

   (C) Ali's wife

3. Who is Azam Javadi?

   (A) Ali's mother

   (B) Ali's wife

   (C) Ali's daughter

4. Who is Omid Azari?

   (A) Ali's brother

   (B) Ali's father

   (C) Ali's son

B Solve the problem. Which solution is best? Circle your opinion.

Ali has a brother. He will live with Ali for two months. What should Ali do?

1. Write his name on the form.

2. Not write his name on the form.

3. Other: _____

2 Fun with vocabulary

A Complete the chart.

an aunt	a baby	a boy	a brother	a daughter	a father	a girl
a grandfather	a grandmother	a husband	a man	a mother	a sister	a son
a teenager	an uncle	a wife	a woman			

Male	Female	Male or female
	an aunt	

Talk with a partner. Compare your answers.

B Write about yourself. Use the words from 2A.

I am _____ , _____ ,

and _____ .

Talk with a partner. Write about your partner.

My partner _____ is _____ ,

_____ , and _____ .

UNIT 4 HEALTH

Lesson A Listening

1 Before you listen

A Look at the picture. What do you see?

B Listen and point: ■ doctor ■ doctor's office ■ medicine ■ nurse ■ patient

CD1, Track 37

Dr. Brown's Office

Mario

Tony

UNIT GOALS
Identify health problems   **Interpret** a medicine label
Identify reasons for a visit to a doctor

2 Listen

A Listen and repeat.

1. doctor   2. doctor's office   3. medicine   4. nurse   5. patient

🔊)) CD1, Track 38

B Listen and circle.

🔊)) CD1, Track 39

1. a.    (b.)

2. a. 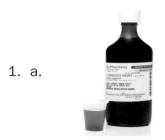   b.

3. a.    b.

4. a.    b.

Listen again. Check your answers.

3 After you listen

Talk with a partner. Point to a picture.
Your partner says the word.

📖 Listen for and identify a patient's request UNIT 4 **45**

Lesson B Parts of the body

1 Vocabulary focus

Listen and repeat.

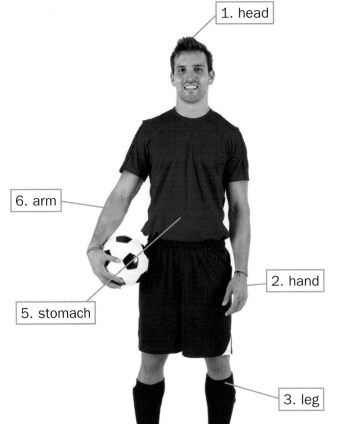

1. head
6. arm
2. hand
5. stomach
3. leg
4. foot

2 Practice

A Read and match.

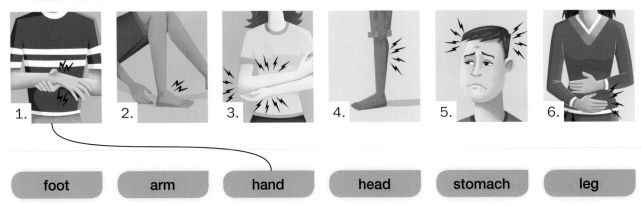

1. 2. 3. 4. 5. 6.

| foot | arm | hand | head | stomach | leg |

B **Listen and repeat.** Then write.

| arm | foot | hand | head | leg | stomach |

CD1, Track 41

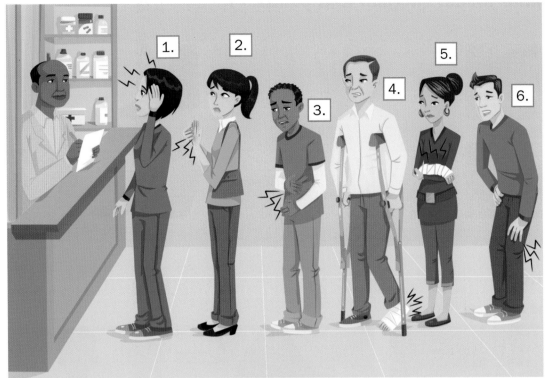

What hurts?

1. My _____head_____.   4. My _____.
2. My _____.   5. My _____.
3. My _____.   6. My _____.

Talk with a partner. Ask and answer.

A What's the matter?

B My **head** hurts.

3 **Communicate**

Talk with a partner.
Act it out. Ask and answer.

> What's the matter?

> My head hurts.

Use vocabulary for parts of the body UNIT 4 **47**

Lesson C My feet hurt.

1 Grammar focus: singular and plural

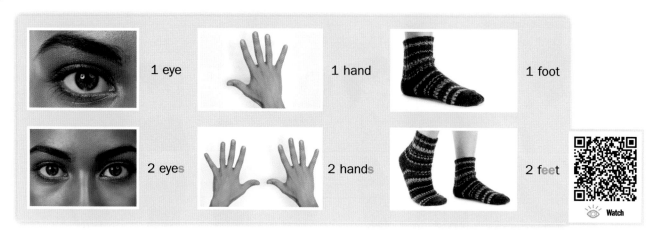

1 eye

2 eyes

1 hand

2 hands

1 foot

2 feet

Watch

2 Practice

A Read and circle. Then write.

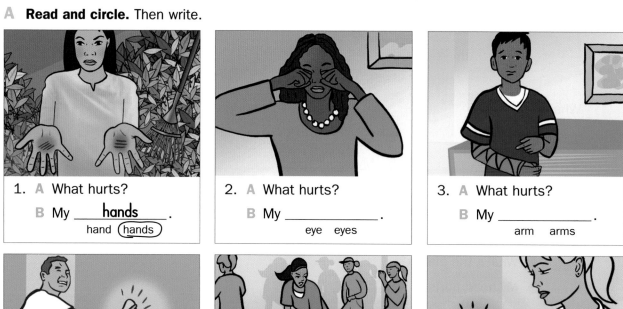

1. **A** What hurts?
    B My ___hands___ .
    hand (hands)

2. **A** What hurts?
    B My _____ .
    eye   eyes

3. **A** What hurts?
    B My _____ .
    arm   arms

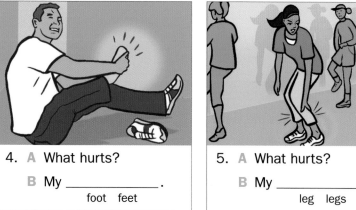

4. **A** What hurts?
    B My _____ .
    foot   feet

5. **A** What hurts?
    B My _____ .
    leg   legs

6. **A** What hurts?
    B My _____ .
    hand   hands

Listen and repeat. Then practice with a partner.

CD1, Track 42

B **Listen and repeat.**

🔊 CD1, Track 43

1. legs

2. hand

3. stomach

4. feet

5. eyes

6. head

Talk with a partner. Act it out. Ask and answer.

A What hurts?

B My **legs**.

A Oh, I'm sorry.

Name	What hurts?
Sasha	head

3 **Communicate**

Talk with your classmates.
Complete the chart.

A What hurts, **Sasha**?

B My **head**.

A Oh, I'm sorry.

📖 Use singular and plural nouns **UNIT 4** **49**

Lesson D Reading

1 Before you read

Talk about the picture.
What do you see?

2 Read

Listen and read.

CD1, Track 44

At the Doctor's Office

Tony and Mario are at the doctor's office. They are patients. Tony's leg hurts. His head hurts, too. He has a headache. Mario's arm hurts. His hands hurt, too. Tony and Mario are not happy. It is not a good day.

3 After you read

Read the sentences. Check (✓) the names.

	Tony	Mario
His arm hurts.		✔
His head hurts.		
His leg hurts.		
His hands hurt.		
He is not happy.		

4 Picture dictionary Health problems

1. a cold

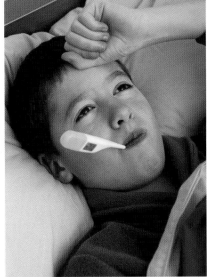

2. a fever

3. a headache

4. a sore throat

5. a stomachache

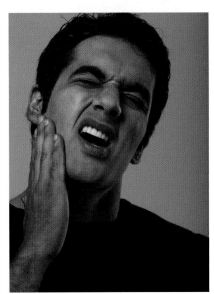

6. a toothache

 A **Listen and repeat.** Look at the Picture dictionary.

B **Talk with a partner.** Act it out. Ask and answer questions.

> **A** What's the matter?
> **B** I have **a cold**.
> **A** Oh, I'm sorry.

CD1, Track 45

1 **Before you write**

Talk with a partner. Check (✓) the reason for the visit.

1.	Name: **Regina**
	Reason for visit:
	☐ cold
	☐ fever
	☐ headache
	☐ sore throat
	☐ stomachache
	✓ toothache

2.	Name: **Isaac**
	Reason for visit:
	☐ cold
	☐ fever
	☐ headache
	☐ sore throat
	☐ stomachache
	☐ toothache

3.	Name: **Joe**
	Reason for visit:
	☐ cold
	☐ fever
	☐ headache
	☐ sore throat
	☐ stomachache
	☐ toothache

4.	Name: **Esperanza**
	Reason for visit:
	☐ cold
	☐ fever
	☐ headache
	☐ sore throat
	☐ stomachache
	☐ toothache

5.	Name: **James**
	Reason for visit:
	☐ cold
	☐ fever
	☐ headache
	☐ sore throat
	☐ stomachache
	☐ toothache

6.	Name: **Sue**
	Reason for visit:
	☐ cold
	☐ fever
	☐ headache
	☐ sore throat
	☐ stomachache
	☐ toothache

2 Write

A **Talk with a partner.** Complete the words.

1. s __o__ re   thr __o__ at
2. c ____ l d
3. s t ____ m a c h a c h e
4. h ____ a d a c h e
5. f ____ v e r
6. t ____ o t h a c h e
7. s ____ r e   h ____ n d

B **Look at page 52.** Then complete the patient sign-in sheet.

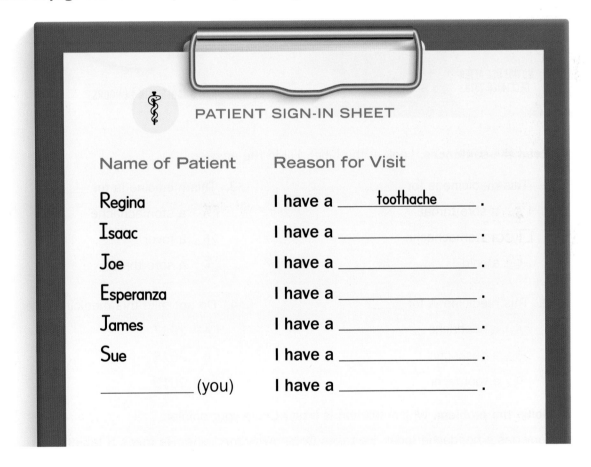

PATIENT SIGN-IN SHEET

Name of Patient   Reason for Visit

Regina   I have a ____toothache____ .

Isaac   I have a _____ .

Joe   I have a _____ .

Esperanza   I have a _____ .

James   I have a _____ .

Sue   I have a _____ .

_____ (you)   I have a _____ .

3 After you write

Talk with a partner. Share your writing.

1 Life-skills reading

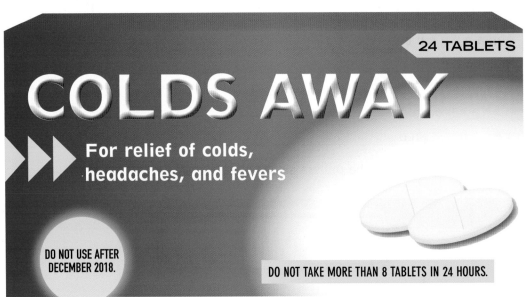

A **Read the sentences.** Look at the label. Fill in the answer.

1. This medicine is for _____ .
   - (A) a sore throat
   - (B) a stomachache
   - (C) a cold

2. This medicine is for _____ .
   - (A) a headache
   - (B) a backache
   - (C) a toothache

3. This medicine is for _____ .
   - (A) a stomachache
   - (B) a fever
   - (C) a sore throat

4. Do not take this medicine after _____ .
   - (A) 2017
   - (B) 2018
   - (C) 2019

B **Solve the problem.** Which solution is best? Circle your opinion.

Tony has a headache today. He takes Colds Away medicine. He takes 8 tablets.
His head still hurts. What should he do?

1. Take another tablet.

2. See a doctor.

3. Other: _____

2 **Fun with vocabulary**

A **Complete the chart.** How many?

	The monster	You
heads	2	1
eyes		
ears		
arms		
legs		
feet		

Talk with a partner. Compare your answers.

B **Write the missing letters.**

p a t __i__ e n t
    1

f ___ e t
   2

s t o ___ a c h
      3

___ u r s e
4

t o o t h a ___ h e
            5

___ o c t o r
6

o f f ___ c e
      7

___ y e
8

Write the letters. Make a word.

___ ___ ___ __i__ ___ ___ ___ ___
 3   2   6   1   5   7   4   8

REVIEW

1 Listening

Read. Then listen and circle.

1. Who is Sonya?

   (a.) Tom's aunt

   b. Tom's brother

2. Who is David?

   a. Tom's aunt

   b. Tom's brother

3. Who is Tina?

   a. Ray's sister

   b. Ray's wife

4. Who is Jay?

   a. Barbara's son

   b. Barbara's brother

5. What hurts?

   a. her hand

   b. her head

6. What hurts?

   a. his leg

   b. his foot

CD1, Track 46

Talk with a partner. Ask and answer.

2 Vocabulary

Write. Complete the story.

cold   doctor's   office   medicine   patients   stomach

A Visit to the Doctor

Marisa and her family are at the ___doctor's office___ .
                                          1

They are _____ . Peter is Marisa's son. His _____
              2   3

hurts. Antonia is Marisa's daughter. She has a _____ .
                                                    4

They need _____ . Marisa isn't happy. She has a
                5

headache!

❸ Grammar

A **Read and circle.** Then write.

1. What hurts? His _____leg_____.
   (leg) legs

2. What hurts? His _____.
   arm   arms

3. What hurts? Her _____.
   hand   hands

4. What hurts? Her _____.
   foot   feet

Dr. Brady

B **Complete the sentences.** Use *do* or *don't*.

A _____Do_____ you have a daughter?
      1

B Yes, we _____.
               2

A _____ you have a son?
      3

B Yes, we _____.
               4

A _____ you have a sister?
      5

B No, I _____.
              6

❹ Pronunciation

A **Listen** to the *e* sound, the *i* sound, and the *u* sound.

e	i	u
re**a**d	f**i**ve	J**u**ne

B **Listen and repeat.**

e	read	need

i	five	write

u	June	rule

Talk with a partner. Say a word. Your partner points. Take turns.

C **Listen and check (✓).**

	e	i	u		e	i	u		e	i	u		e	i	u		e	i	u
1.		✓		2.				3.				4.				5.			

🔊 CD1, Track 47

🔊 CD1, Track 48

🔊 CD1, Track 49

UNIT 5 AROUND TOWN

Lesson A Listening

1 Before you listen

A Look at the picture. What do you see?

B Listen and point: ■ bank ■ library ■ restaurant ■ school
■ street ■ supermarket

◀)) CD1, Track 50

UNIT GOALS
Identify places around town **Describe** places on a map
Complete a map and write about it

2 Listen

A Listen and repeat.

1. bank   2. library   3. restaurant

4. school   5. street   6. supermarket

◄)) CD1, Track 51

◄)) CD1, Track 52

B Listen and circle.

1. (a.) 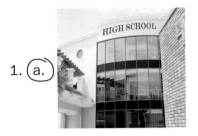   b.

2. a.    b.

3. a.    b.

4. a.    b.

Listen again. Check your answers.

3 After you listen

Talk with a partner. Point to a picture.
Your partner says the word.

1 Vocabulary focus

Listen and repeat.

CD1, Track 53

1. pharmacy

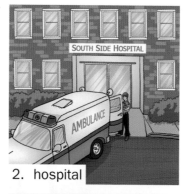
2. hospital

3. laundromat

4. post office

5. movie theater

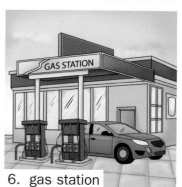
6. gas station

2 Practice

A Read and match.

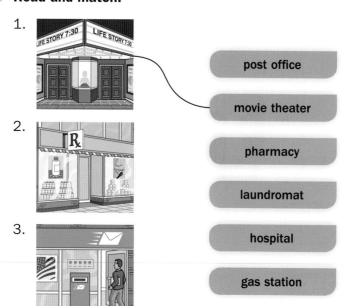

post office

movie theater

pharmacy

laundromat

hospital

gas station

B **Listen and repeat.** Then write.

 CD1, Track 54

| gas station | hospital | laundromat |
| movie theater | pharmacy | post office |

1. Minh

2. Alan

3. Mr. Lopez

4. Paula

5. Jackie

6. Isabel

Name	Place	Name	Place
1. Minh	movie theater	4. Paula	
2. Alan		5. Jackie	
3. Mr. Lopez		6. Isabel	

Talk with a partner. Ask and answer.

A   Where's **Minh**?

B   At the **movie theater**.

3 Communicate

Work in a group. Play a game.
Ask and guess.

A   Where is **he**?

B   At the **movie theater**?

C   That's right!

Lesson C The school is on Main Street.

1 Grammar focus: *on, next to, across from, between*

Watch

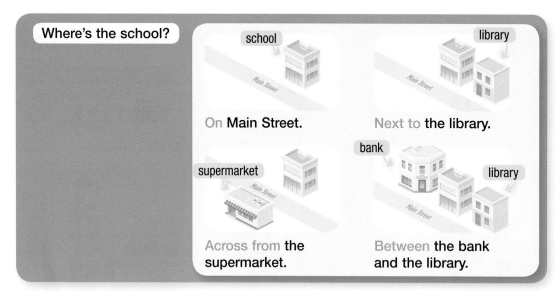

Where's the school?

school
On **Main Street.**

library
Next to **the library.**

supermarket
Across from **the supermarket.**

bank   library
Between **the bank and the library.**

2 Practice

A **Read and circle.** Then write.

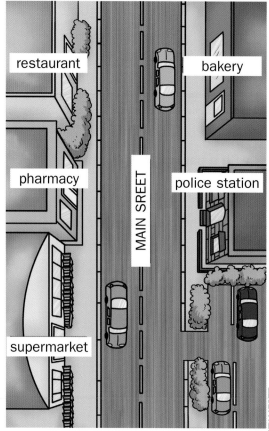

restaurant   bakery

pharmacy   police station

MAIN SREET

supermarket

1. **A** Where's the pharmacy?

   B ___**Between**___ the restaurant
   (Between) Across from
   and the supermarket.

2. **A** Where's the supermarket?

   B _____ Main Street.
   Across from   On

3. **A** Where's the restaurant?

   B _____ the pharmacy.
   Between   Next to

4. **A** Where's the bakery?

   B _____ the restaurant.
   Next to   Across from

5. **A** Where's the police station?

   B _____ the bakery.
   On   Next to

Listen and repeat.
Then practice with a partner.

CD1, Track 55

B **Listen and repeat.**

🔊 CD1, Track 56

1. next to

2. across from

3. between

4. on

5. next to

6. across from

Talk with a partner. Ask and answer.

A Excuse me. Where's the **bank**?

B **Next to the supermarket.**

A Thanks.

3 **Communicate**

Talk with a partner. Play a game.
Ask and guess.

A Where are you?

B **Next to the supermarket.**

A At the **bank**?

B Yes, that's right.

Lesson D Reading

1 Before you read

Talk about the picture.
What do you see?

2 Read

Listen and read.

CD1, Track 57

 Notice from Riverside Library

Come and visit Riverside Library. The new library opens today.
The library is on Main Street. It is across from Riverside Adult
School. It is next to K and P Supermarket. It is between K and
P Supermarket and Rosie's Restaurant. The library is open
from 9:00 to 5:00, Monday, Wednesday, and Friday.

3 After you read

Complete the map. Share your map with a partner.

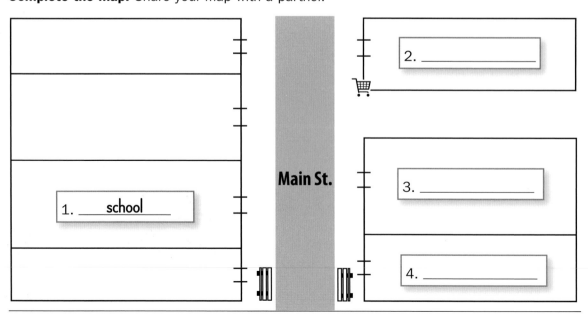

1. _____school_____

2. _____

3. _____

4. _____

Main St.

4 **Picture dictionary** Transportation

1. by bicycle

2. by bus

3. by car

4. by taxi

5. by train

6. on foot

A **Listen and repeat.** Look at the Picture dictionary.

B **Talk with your classmates.** Complete the chart.

A **Ben**, how do you get
to school?

B **By car.**

CD1, Track 58

Name	Transportation
Ben	by car

Lesson E Writing

1 Before you write

A Talk with a partner. Complete the words.

1. s u p e r m a r __k__ e t

2. p ____ a r m a c y

3. p o s t   o f ____ i c e

4. r e s ____ a u r a n t

5. l i ____ r a r y

6. s ____ h o o l

B Talk with a partner. Look at the map. Complete the story.

Reed Street

    Donna lives on Reed _____ Street _____ . She lives near a big
                     1

supermarket. The supermarket is next to a _____ .
                                   2

A _____ is across from the supermarket. A
         3

p_____ is on Reed Street, too. It is across from
       4

the _____ . A _____ is between the
      5   6

restaurant and the library.

2 Write

A Draw a map of your street.

B Write about your street.

1. I live on _____ .
2. I live near a _____ .
3. A _____ is across from a _____ .
4. A _____ is between the _____ and the _____ .

3 After you write

Listen to your partner. Draw your partner's street.

Lesson F Another view

1 Life-skills reading

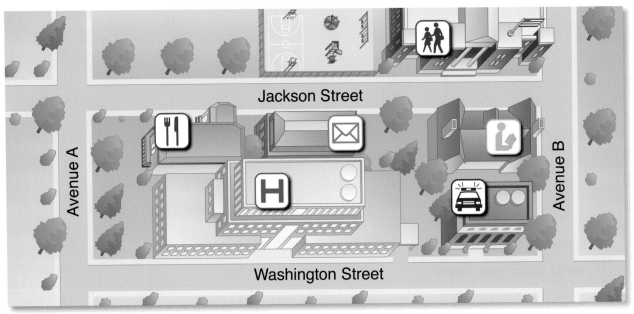

A Read the sentences. Look at the map. Fill in the answer.

1. The hospital is _____.
   - (A) on Jackson Street
   - (B) on Washington Street
   - (C) on Avenue B

2. The post office is _____.
   - (A) next to the police station
   - (B) next to the school
   - (C) next to the restaurant

3. The post office is _____.
   - (A) between the restaurant and the library
   - (B) across from the library
   - (C) on Washington Street

4. The hospital is _____.
   - (A) across from the school
   - (B) next to the police station
   - (C) between the restaurant and the school

B Solve the problem. Which solution is best? Circle your answer.

Where's the library? Eva doesn't know. What can she do?

1. Look at a map.

2. Go home.

3. Other: _____

2 **Fun with vocabulary**

A Read and match.

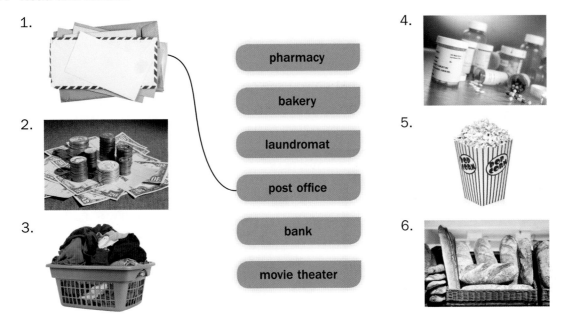

1.

pharmacy

bakery

laundromat

post office

bank

movie theater

2.

3.

4.

5.

6.

Talk with a partner. Check your answers.

B Circle the words in the puzzle.

bicycle   bus   car   foot   taxi   train

k	f	f	o	o	t	c	s
v	x	a	m	b	r	a	m
k	a	o	t	r	a	i	n
t	a	x	i	s	i	g	t
k	a	v	i	b	u	s	n
b	i	c	y	c	l	e	e
x	r	w	c	a	r	k	b

UNIT 6 TIME

Lesson A Listening

1 Before you listen

A Look at the picture. What do you see?

B Listen and point: ■ 7:00 ■ 9:00 ■ 10:00 ■ 10:30
■ 2:30 ■ 6:30

CD2, Track 02

UNIT GOALS
Read clock time **Make** a schedule
Identify parts of an invitation

2 Listen

A Listen and repeat.

1. 7:00   2. 9:00   3. 10:00
4. 10:30   5. 2:30   6. 6:30

CD2, Track 03

B Listen and circle.

CD2, Track 04

1. a.    b.

2. a.    b.

3. a.    b.

4. a.    b.

Listen again. Check your answers.

3 After you listen

Talk with a partner.
Point to a picture and
ask. Your partner says
the time.

USEFUL LANGUAGE
Say times like this.
3:00 = *three o'clock*
6:30 = *six-thirty*

What time is it?   It's 10 o'clock.

Lesson B Events

1 Vocabulary focus

Listen and repeat.

September

Sunday	Monday	Tuesday	Wednesday	Thursday	Friday	Saturday
			1	2	3	4
5	6	7 1. appointment 1:30	8 3. class	9	10 2. meeting 3:30	11 4. movie
12	13	14	15 page 6 8:30	16	17	18 7:30
19 5. party	20	21	22 6. TV show	23	24	25
26 5:00	27	28	29 4:30	30		

2 Practice

A Read and match.

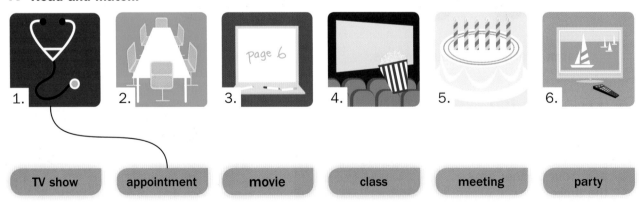

| TV show | appointment | movie | class | meeting | party |

B **Listen and repeat.** Then write.

1.

Town Haircuts

APPOINTMENT INFO:

Day & Time: Friday 1:30

Haircut with: Nick

2.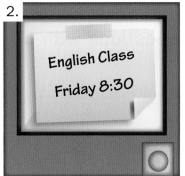

English Class
Friday 8:30

3.

4:30 **Friday**

Channel 3 One Life, One Love
1 hour

Channel 5 Dinosaurs
30 minutes

Channel 8 Afternoon Special
1 hour

🔊 CD2, Track 06

4.

RIVERSIDE SCHOOL
PTA MEETING
SATURDAY 3:00

5.

ATTACK FROM VENUS!!
NOW PLAYING: SATURDAY 9:00

6.

You're Invited!
Gina's Birthday Party
Saturday 5:00

Event	Time	Day
appointment	1:30	Friday
TV show		
movie		

Event	Time	Day
class		
party		
meeting		

Talk with a partner. Ask and answer.

A What time is the **appointment**?

B At **1:30** on **Friday**.

③ **Communicate**

Complete the chart. Write a time and day for each event.
Then talk with your classmates.

Event	Time	Day
movie	7:30	Saturday
TV show		
party		
meeting		

A What time is the **movie**?

B At **7:30** on **Saturday**.

Lesson C Is your class at 11:00?

1 Grammar focus: Yes / No questions with *be*

QUESTIONS			ANSWERS	
Is	your class	at 11:00?	Yes, No,	it is. it isn't.

isn't = is not

Watch

2 Practice

A **Read and circle.** Then write.

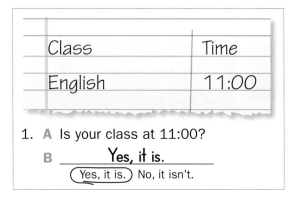

Class	Time
English	11:00

1. **A** Is your class at 11:00?
   B _____Yes, it is._____
   (Yes, it is.)   No, it isn't.

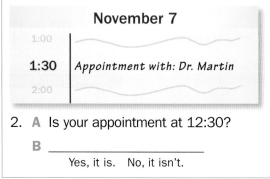

November 7

1:00	
1:30	*Appointment with: Dr. Martin*
2:00	

2. **A** Is your appointment at 12:30?
   B _____
   Yes, it is.   No, it isn't.

The Paramount Concert Hall
Toni Tucker
Tonight Only! 8:30 p.m.

3. **A** Is your concert at 8:00?
   B _____
   Yes, it is.   No, it isn't.

THE LOST CLUES
6:00

4. **A** Is your movie at 6:00?
   B _____
   Yes, it is.   No, it isn't.

Sammy's Birthday Party
4:00

5. **A** Is your party at 4:00?
   B _____
   Yes, it is.   No, it isn't.

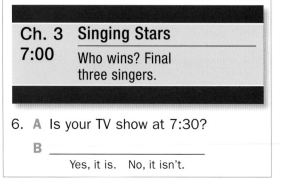

Ch. 3 7:00	**Singing Stars** Who wins? Final three singers.

6. **A** Is your TV show at 7:30?
   B _____
   Yes, it is.   No, it isn't.

Listen and repeat. Then practice with a partner.

CD2, Track 07

B **Read and match.**

April

2 Monday	3:30 Doctor's appointment	5 Thursday	8:00 Movie with my sister
3 Tuesday	6:30 English class	6 Friday	7:30 Birthday party
4 Wednesday	12:00 Meeting at work	7 Saturday	9:00 Concert: Salsa music
		8 Sunday	

1. appointment — seven-thirty
2. class — six-thirty
3. meeting — three-thirty
4. movie — nine o'clock
5. party — twelve o'clock
6. concert — eight o'clock

Talk with a partner. Ask and answer.

A Is your **appointment** on **Monday**?

B **Yes, it is.**

A Is your **appointment** at **7:00**?

B **No, it isn't. It's at 3:30.**

3 Communicate

Complete the chart. Write an event and time for each day.
Then talk with a partner.

appointment　class　concert　meeting　party

Monday	Tuesday	Wednesday	Thursday	Friday
class – 5:00				

A Is your **class** on **Tuesday**?

B **No, it isn't. It's on Monday.**

A Is your **class** at **5:00**?

B **Yes, it is.**

Lesson D Reading

1 Before you read

Talk about the picture.
What do you see?

2 Read

Listen and read.

🔊 CD2, Track 08

Teresa's Day

Teresa is busy today. Her meeting with her friend Joan is at 10:00 in the morning. Her doctor's appointment is at 1:00 in the afternoon. Her favorite TV show is at 4:30. Her class is at 6:30 in the evening. Her uncle's birthday party is also at 6:30. Oh, no! What will she do?

3 After you read

Write the answers.

1. What time is Teresa's meeting? _____At 10:00_____.

2. What time is Teresa's TV show? _____.

3. What time is Teresa's class? _____.

4. Is Teresa's appointment at 4:00? _____.

5. Is her uncle's party at 6:30? _____.

4 Picture dictionary Times of the day

1. in the morning

2. in the afternoon

3. in the evening

12:00 p.m.

4. at noon

5. at night

12:00 a.m.

6. at midnight

A **Listen and repeat.** Look at the Picture dictionary.

B **Talk with a partner.** Complete the chart.
Check (✓) the time of the day.

A It's at **12:00 p.m.**

B **At noon?**

A Right.

CD2, Track 09

USEFUL LANGUAGE
a.m. = from midnight to noon
p.m. = from noon to midnight

Event	In the morning	In the afternoon	In the evening	At noon	At midnight
12:00 p.m.				✓	
3:00 p.m.					
6:00 a.m.					
12:00 a.m.					
6:00 p.m.					

1 Before you write

A **Talk with a partner.** Complete the words.

1. m o v <u>i</u> <u>e</u>
2. c l a ____ ____
3. a p p ____ ____ n t m e n t
4. p ____ ____ t y
5. T V ____ ____ o w
6. m ____ ____ t i n g

B **Talk with a partner.** Look at the memo. Complete the story.

MEMO

TIME	EVENT
8:00 a.m.	meeting – daughter's school
12:00 p.m.	doctor's appointment
1:30 p.m.	class
6:00 p.m.	party – son's class
8:00 p.m.	TV show

My Busy Day

Today is a busy day. My ____meeting____ at my daughter's school is at
                              1
8:00 in the morning. Then my doctor's _____ is at noon. My English
                                              2
_____ is at 1:30. What time is my son's class _____? Oh, yes.
     3   4
At 6:00 in the evening. Dinner with my family is at 7:00. And my favorite TV
_____ is at 8:00 at night. It's a very busy day.
     5

2 Write

A **Complete the memo.** Write four times and four events for you.

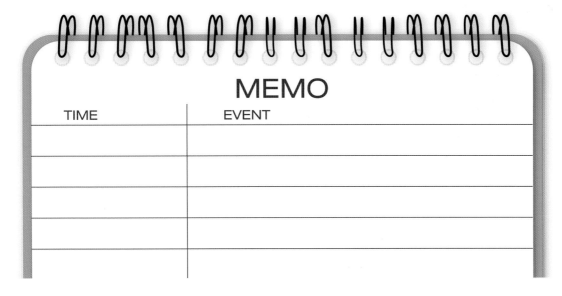

B **Write about your day.**

My Busy Day

Today is a busy day.

My _____ is at _____.

My _____ is at _____.

My _____ is at _____.

And my _____ is at _____.

It's a very busy day.

3 After you write

Talk with a partner. Share your writing.

1 Life-skills reading

A **Read the sentences.** Look at the invitation. Fill in the answer.

It's a party!

Lily is 50! It's a surprise.
Don't tell her.

When: Saturday, October 2
What time: 8:00 p.m.
Where: Katya and Alex's house
874 Lake Road
RSVP: Call Katya at 555-6188.

1. Who is the party for?
   Ⓐ Lily
   Ⓑ Katya and Alex
   Ⓒ Katya

2. When is the party?
   Ⓐ in the morning
   Ⓑ in the afternoon
   Ⓒ at night

3. What time is the party?
   Ⓐ 2:00 p.m.
   Ⓑ 4:00 p.m.
   Ⓒ 8:00 p.m.

4. What day is the party?
   Ⓐ Friday
   Ⓑ Saturday
   Ⓒ Sunday

B **Solve the problem.** Which solution is best? Circle your opinion.

Teresa can't go to the party. What should she do?

1. Call Lily.

2. Call 555-6188.

3. Other: _____

2 Fun with vocabulary

A **Write times on the clocks.**
Talk with a partner. Listen and write your partner's times.

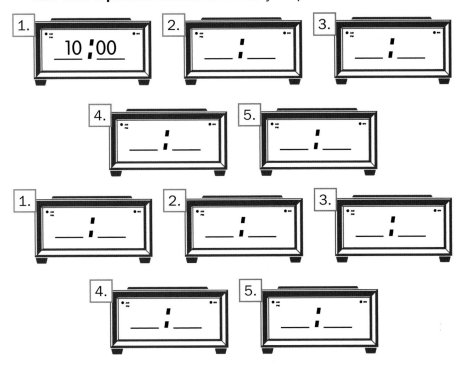

1. 10 : 00
2. ___ : ___
3. ___ : ___
4. ___ : ___
5. ___ : ___

1. ___ : ___
2. ___ : ___
3. ___ : ___
4. ___ : ___
5. ___ : ___

A What time is it?

B It's **10:00**.

B **Write the missing letters.**

<u>d</u> a y
1

___ o v i e
2

at n o o ___
3

at n i g ___ t
4

in the e v e n ___ n g
5

in the a f ___ e r n o o n
6

in the m o r n i n ___
7

a p p o ___ n t m e n t
8

What time is it? Write the letters below.

___ ___ <u>d</u> ___ ___ ___ ___ ___
2   8   1   3   5   7   4   6

REVIEW

1 Listening

Read. Then listen and circle.

1. Is the meeting on Friday?

   (a.) Yes, it is.

   b. No, it isn't.

2. What time is the meeting?

   a. at 2:30

   b. at 10:30

3. What time is the appointment?

   a. at 2:00

   b. at 4:00

4. Where's the school?

   a. next to the bank

   b. across from the bank

5. Where's the movie theater?

   a. between the supermarket and the pharmacy

   b. next to the supermarket

6. Is the movie at 7:30?

   a. Yes, it is.

   b. No, it isn't.

CD2, Track 10

Talk with a partner. Ask and answer.

2 Vocabulary

Write. Complete the story.

afternoon   class   8:30   hospital   meeting

Tan's Day

Tan's English _____class_____ is at _____ in the morning.
                      1   2

His _____ is at 1:00 in the _____. The
         3   4

meeting is at the _____, next to the school.
                         5

It's a busy day.

3 Grammar

A Read and circle. Then write.

1. The library is _____across from_____ the bank.

    on (across from)

2. The post office is _____ the bank and the library.

    next to   between

3. The restaurant is _____ Main Street.

    on   between

4. The hospital is _____ the gas station.

    across from   between

B Read the memo and answer. Write *Yes, it is* or *No, it isn't*.

1. Is the movie at 6:00?

    _____No, it isn't_____ .

2. Is the class at 9:00?

    _____ .

3. Is the meeting in the morning?

    _____ .

4. Is the appointment in the afternoon?

    _____ .

Morning
9:00 class
Afternoon
2:00 – meeting with Ms. Morales
4:30 – appointment with Dr. Morgan
Evening
6:30 – movie

4 Pronunciation

A Listen to the *a* sound and the *o* sound.

a	o
at	on

CD2, Track 11

B Listen and repeat.

a	at	class	map

o	on	clock	not

CD2, Track 12

Talk with a partner. Say a word. Your partner points. Take turns.

C Listen and check (✓).

	a	o		a	o		a	o		a	o		a	o
1.		✓	2.			3.			4.			5.		

CD2, Track 13

UNIT 7 SHOPPING

Lesson A Listening

1 Before you listen

A Look at the picture. What do you see?

B Listen and point: ▪ a dress ▪ pants ▪ a shirt ▪ shoes
▪ socks ▪ a T-shirt

CD2, Track 14

SUMMER SALE!

THE CLOTHES PLACE

$19.00

$1.99

$39.99

$27.00

$24.99

$10.99

Rose

Samuel

UNIT GOALS
Identify prices **Interpret** a receipt
Complete a shopping list

2 Listen

A Listen and repeat.

1. a dress   2. pants   3. a shirt
4. shoes   5. socks   6. a T-shirt

B Listen and circle.

 CD2, Track 15

CD2, Track 16

1. (a.)    b.

2. a.    b.

3. a.    b.

4. a.    b.

Listen again. Check your answers.

3 After you listen

Talk with a partner. Point to a picture.
Your partner says the word.

A dress.

📖 Listen for and identify clothing items **UNIT 7** **85**

Lesson B Clothing

1 Vocabulary focus

Listen and repeat.

Back-to-School Sale

1	2	3
a tie $10.00	a blouse $19.99	a sweater $29.99

4	5	6
a skirt $24.99	a jacket $89.99	a raincoat $39.99

2 Practice

A Read and match.

1.   2.   3.   4.   5.   6.

a tie   a blouse   a jacket   a skirt   a raincoat   a sweater

B **Listen and repeat.** Then write.

blouse	jacket	raincoat	skirt	sweater	tie

🔊)) CD2, Track 18

1. The ___tie___ is $9.99.   2. The _____ is $26.95.   3. The _____ is $35.95.

4. The _____ is $39.99.   5. The _____ is $48.99.   6. The _____ is $25.95.

Talk with a partner. Ask and answer.

   A How much is the **tie**?

B **$9.99.**

> **USEFUL LANGUAGE**
> $9.99 = *nine ninety-nine*
> or
> *nine dollars and ninety-nine cents*

3 **Communicate**

Write prices. Your partner asks the price. You answer.

$ ___24.99___ $ _____ $ _____ $ _____ $ _____

   A How much is the **skirt**?

B **$24.99.**

Lesson C How much are the shoes?

1 Grammar focus: *How much is? / How much are?*

QUESTIONS			ANSWERS
How much	is are	the shirt? the shoes?	$15.99. $68.95.

Watch

2 Practice

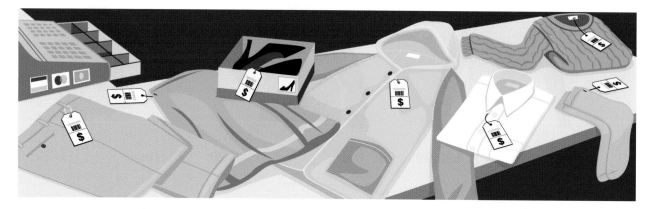

A Read and circle. Then write.

1. **A** How much ___**are**___ the pants?
   _{is (are)}
   B $24.99.

2. **A** How much _____ the skirt?
   _{is   are}
   B $18.99.

3. **A** How much _____ the raincoat?
   _{is   are}
   B $16.95.

4. **A** How much _____ the shoes?
   _{is   are}
   B $58.99.

5. **A** How much _____ the sweater?
   _{is   are}
   B $31.99.

6. **A** How much _____ the socks?
   _{is   are}
   B $5.95.

Listen and repeat. Then practice with a partner.

CD2, Track 19

B **Listen and repeat.** Then write the price.

🔊 **CD2, Track** 20

1.	T-shirt	$2.00
2.	shoes	
3.	jacket	
4.	sweater	
5.	raincoat	
6.	pants	
7.	socks	
8.	blouse	

Talk with a partner. Ask and answer.

💬 **A** How much **is the T-shirt**?
B $2.00.
A $2.00? Thanks.

💬 **A** How much **are the shoes**?
B $3.00.
A $3.00? Thanks.

③ Communicate

Write prices. Your partner asks the price. You answer.

$ __5.00__ $ _____ $ _____ $ _____ $ _____

💬 **A** How much **are the socks**?
B $5.00.

Lesson D Reading

1 Before you read

Talk about the picture.
What do you see?

2 Read

Listen and read.

● ● ●

From:	Rose	Reply Forward
To:	Patty	
Subject:	Shopping	

Hi Patty,

This morning, Samuel and I are going to The Clothes Place. Samuel needs blue pants. He needs a tie, too. I need a red dress and black shoes. Dresses are on sale. They're $49.99. Shoes are on sale, too. They're $34.99. That's good.

Call you later,
Rose

🔊 CD2, Track 21

3 After you read

Read and match.

1.

Samuel needs blue pants.

Samuel needs a tie.

Dresses are on sale.

Shoes are on sale.

2.

3.

4.

4 **Picture dictionary** Colors

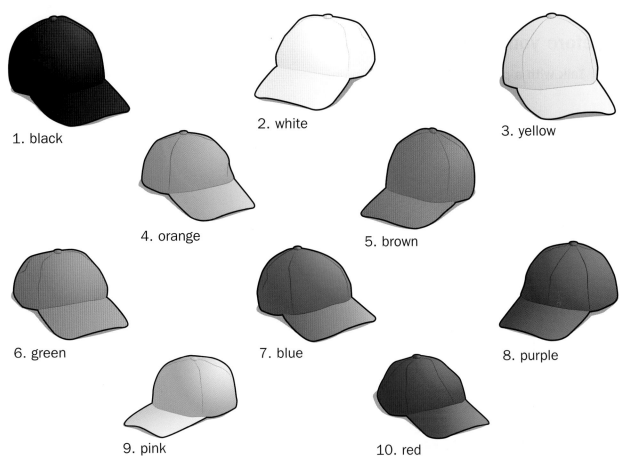

1. black

2. white

3. yellow

4. orange

5. brown

6. green

7. blue

8. purple

9. pink

10. red

A **Listen and repeat.** Look at the Picture dictionary.

B **Talk with a partner.** Look around your classroom. Ask and answer.

 A What color is **her sweater**?

B **Blue.**

 A What color are **his shoes**?

B **Brown.**

 CD2, Track 22

C **Talk with a partner.** Choose four classmates. Complete the chart.

Name	red	yellow	green	black	white	brown	blue
Eliza	sweater	socks			blouse		

Lesson E Writing

1 Before you write

A Talk with a partner. Complete the words.

Shopping list

1. _s_ _k_ i r t
2. ___ ___ e s s
3. ___ ___ o e s
4. ___ ___ o u s e
5. ___ ___ e a t e r
6. T- ___ ___ i r t

B Talk with a partner. Look at the picture. Complete the story.

Sun Mi and her children are shopping today. They

need clothes for school. Sun Mi needs a ___dress___ and
                                            1

_____ . Her son Roger needs a _____ and a
      2   3

_____ . Her daughter Emily needs a _____ and
      4   5

a _____ .
        6

2 Write

A Complete the shopping list for Sun Mi's family.

Name	Clothing
Sun Mi:	a dress,
Emily:	
Roger:	

B Circle the clothes you and your family need.

a blouse	socks	a tie	a dress
a sweater	a jacket	a skirt	a raincoat
a T-shirt	a shirt	shoes	pants

C Write a shopping list for your family.

Name	Clothing

3 After you write

Talk with a partner. Share your writing.

Lesson F Another view

1 Life-skills reading

THE
Clothes
PLACE

271 Center Street
Tampa, Florida 33601
(813) 555-7200

Shoes	$29.99
T-shirt	$7.99
Subtotal:	$37.98
7% Tax:	$2.66
Total:	$40.64

Thank you for shopping at
The Clothes Place.
Have a nice day!

A **Read the sentences.** Look at the receipt. Fill in the answer.

1. What is The Clothes Place?

   Ⓐ clothing store

   Ⓑ supermarket

   Ⓒ laundromat

2. What's the phone number?

   Ⓐ 555-0072

   Ⓑ 555-7200

   Ⓒ 813

3. How much are the shoes?

   Ⓐ $29.99

   Ⓑ $19.99

   Ⓒ $40.64

4. How much is the tax?

   Ⓐ $40.64

   Ⓑ $37.98

   Ⓒ $2.66

B **Solve the problem.** Which solution is best? Circle your opinion.

Jimmy wants a black T-shirt. A black T-shirt is $14.99. A blue T-shirt is $7.99.
What should his mother buy?

1. a black T-shirt

2. a blue T-shirt

3. Other: _____

2 Fun with vocabulary

Write the words in the puzzle. Some words go across (→).
Some words go down (↓).

Across →

1.

9.

5.

10.

8.

Down ↓

2.

5.

3.

6.

4.

7.

1 Before you listen

A Look at the picture. What do you see?

B Listen and point: ▪ cashier ▪ custodian ▪ mechanic ▪ receptionist ▪ salesperson ▪ server

🔊 CD2, Track 23

UNIT GOALS
Identify jobs   **Identify** job duties
Interpret help wanted ads

2 Listen

A Listen and repeat.

1. cashier
2. custodian
3. mechanic
4. receptionist
5. salesperson
6. server

CD2, Track 24

CD2, Track 25

B Listen and circle.

1. a.    b.

2. a.    b.

3. a.    b.

4. a.    b.

Listen again. Check your answers.

3 After you listen

Talk with a partner. Point to a picture.
Your partner says the word.

Lesson B Job duties

1 Vocabulary focus

Listen and repeat.

CD2, Track 26

1. She answers the phone.

2. She counts money.

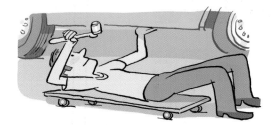

3. He fixes cars.

4. He cleans buildings.

5. She sells clothes.

6. He serves food.

2 Practice

A Read and match.

1. A receptionist   sells clothes.

2. A salesperson   cleans buildings.

3. A cashier   answers the phone.

4. A server   fixes cars.

5. A custodian   serves food.

6. A mechanic   counts money.

B **Listen and repeat.** Then write.

| answers the phone | cleans buildings | counts money |
| fixes cars | sells clothes | serves food |

CD2, Track 27

Stephanie

Sandra

DOCTOR'S OFFICE

Alba

Tim

Oscar

Ahmad

Name	Duty	Name	Duty
1. Sandra	She _____counts money_____ .	4. Oscar	He _____ .
2. Stephanie	She _____ .	5. Tim	He _____ .
3. Alba	She _____ .	6. Ahmad	He _____ .

Talk with a partner. Ask and answer.

A What does **Sandra** do?

B **She counts money.**

3 Communicate

Talk with your classmates. Ask and answer.

A What do you do?

B I'm a **cashier. I count money.**

USEFUL LANGUAGE
What do you do? =
What's your job?

Lesson C Does he sell clothes?

1 Grammar focus: *does* and *doesn't*

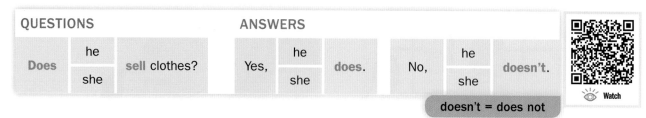

QUESTIONS			ANSWERS					
Does	he / she	sell clothes?	Yes,	he / she	does.	No,	he / she	doesn't.

Watch

doesn't = does not

2 Practice

A **Read and circle.** Then write.

1. **A** Does he serve food?
   B No, he ___**doesn't**___.
   does (doesn't)

2. **A** Does he clean buildings?
   B No, he _____.
   does   doesn't

3. **A** Does she answer the phone?
   B Yes, she _____.
   does   doesn't

4. **A** Does he sell clothes?
   B Yes, he _____.
   does   doesn't

5. **A** Does she fix cars?
   B No, she _____.
   does   doesn't

Listen and repeat. Then practice with a partner.

CD2, Track 28

B **Listen and repeat.** Then write.

CD2, Track 29

1. A ___Does___ he ___sell___ clothes?
   B ___No___, he ___doesn't___.

2. A _____ he _____ cars?
   B _____, he _____.

3. A _____ he _____ buildings?
   B _____, he _____.

4. A _____ he _____ food?
   B _____, he _____.

5. A _____ he _____ money?
   B _____, he _____.

6. A _____ he _____ the phone?
   B _____, he _____.

Talk with a partner. Ask and guess his job.

cashier	custodian	mechanic
receptionist	salesperson	server

A What's his job?

B He's a _____.

3 **Communicate**

Talk with your classmates. Play a game.
Ask and guess.

A Do you **sell clothes**?

B **No.**

A Do you **fix cars**?

B **Yes.**

A You're a **mechanic**?

B **Yes, that's right.**

Lesson D Reading

1 Before you read

Talk about the picture.
What do you see?

2 Read

Listen and read.

CD2, Track 30

EMPLOYEE of the MONTH

Sara Lopez

Congratulations, Sara Lopez – Employee of the Month! Sara is a salesperson. She sells clothes. Sara's whole family works here at Shop Smart. Her father is a custodian, and her mother is a receptionist. Her uncle Eduardo is a server. He serves food. Her sister Lucy is a cashier. She counts money. Her brother Leo fixes cars. He's a mechanic. Everybody in the store knows the Lopez family!

3 After you read

Write the job and the job duty.

1.
Name	Job
Leo Lopez	mechanic

Job duty
He fixes cars. $hop $mart

2.
Name	Job
Lucy Lopez	

Job duty
_____ $hop $mart

3.
Name	Job
Eduardo Lopez	

Job duty
_____ $hop $mart

4.
Name	Job
Sara Lopez	

Job duty
_____ $hop $mart

4 **Picture dictionary** Jobs

1. bus driver

2. homemaker

3. painter

4. plumber

5. teacher's aide

6. truck driver

A **Listen and repeat.** Look at the Picture dictionary.

B **Talk with a partner.** Point and ask. Your partner answers.

A What does **he** do?

B **He's a teacher's aide.**

CD2, Track 31

1 Before you write

A **Talk with a partner.** Check (✓) the job duty.

	Counts money	Drives a bus	Cleans buildings	Answers the phone	Serves food
cashier	✓				
custodian					
server					
bus driver					
receptionist					

B **Talk with a partner.** Complete the words.

1. s a l e s p __e__ __r__ s o n
2. s e l l s ____ ____ o t h e s
3. m e ____ ____ a n i c
4. f i x ____ ____ c a r s
5. a n ____ ____ e r s t h e p h o n e
6. c ____ ____ n t s m o n e y

C **Read the letter.**

Dear Grandpa,

How are you? We are all well here. Luis and Maria have new jobs! Luis is a server. He serves food. Maria is a receptionist. She answers the phone. I'm a homemaker. I work at home. Write soon.

Love,
Rosa

2 Write

A **Talk with a partner.** Complete the letter. Use the words from 1B.

Dear Grandma,

How are you? We are all well here. Janie and Walter have new jobs!

Janie is a __salesperson__ . She _____ clothes. She also _____
₁   2   3

the phone at work, and she _____ money. Walter is a _____ . He
                          4   5

_____ cars.
    6

Write soon.

                                Love,
                                Meg

B **Write about your family and friends.** Write about their jobs.

My _____friend's_____ name is _____Sandra_____ .
She is a _____receptionist_____ . She _____answers the phone_____ .

1. My _____'s name is _____ .
He is a _____ . He _____ .

2. My _____'s name is _____ .
She is a _____ . She _____ .

3. My _____'s name is _____ .
_____ is a _____ .
_____ .

3 After you write

Talk with a partner. Share your writing.

Lesson F Another view

1 Life-skills reading

Help Wanted

JOB A **Salesperson**
$15.00 an hour
Monday and Wednesday
Call 555-1188

JOB B **Painter**
Acme Paint Company
Call 555-8491
Part-time work

JOB C **Cashier**
$12.00 an hour
Shop Smart
Email: ShopSmart@cup.org

JOB D **Bus Driver**
City Bus Company
Work mornings
Call evenings
555-7654

A **Read the sentences.** Look at the ads. Fill in the answer.

1. What is Job A for?

   Ⓐ cashier

   Ⓑ receptionist

   Ⓒ salesperson

2. What is Job B for?

   Ⓐ driver

   Ⓑ painter

   Ⓒ plumber

3. You want the cashier job. What should you do?

   Ⓐ write to Shop Smart

   Ⓑ go to Shop Smart

   Ⓒ call Shop Smart

4. You want the bus driver job. What should you do?

   Ⓐ call in the morning

   Ⓑ call in the afternoon

   Ⓒ call in the evening

B **Solve the problem.** Which solution is best? Circle your opinion.

Ana wants to apply for Job C, but she doesn't have a computer. What should she do?

1. Use a computer at the library.

2. Borrow a friend's computer.

3. Other: _____

2 Fun with vocabulary

A Read and match.

1.
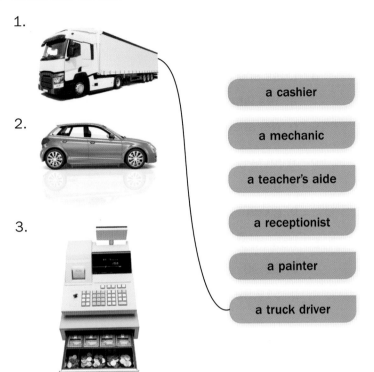

2.

3.

a cashier

a mechanic

a teacher's aide

a receptionist

a painter

a truck driver

4.

5.

6.

Talk with a partner. Check your answers.

B Circle the words in the puzzle.

answer	cashier	clean	count	custodian
fix	mechanic	sell	server	

```
t  (f  i  x)  a  b  c  o  u  n  t  q

f  g  m  e  c  h  a  n  i  c  r  o

s  e  r  v  e  r  c  c  l  e  a  n

d  s  e  a  n  s  w  e  r  u  b  a

s  e  l  l  l  c  a  s  h  i  e  r

t  r  c  u  s  t  o  d  i  a  n  r
```

REVIEW

1 Listening

Read. Then listen and circle.

1. What does Chul do?
   a. He's a cashier.
   b. He's a custodian.

2. Does he serve food?
   a. Yes, he does.
   b. No, he doesn't.

3. What does Luz do?
   a. She's a salesperson.
   b. She's a receptionist.

4. Does she answer the phone?
   a. Yes, she does.
   b. No, she doesn't.

5. What color are the pants?
   a. blue
   b. green

6. How much are the pants?
   a. $9.99
   b. $19.99

CD2, Track 32

Talk with a partner. Ask and answer.

2 Vocabulary

Write. Complete the story.

cars   clothes   mechanic $9.99   salesperson   shirt

A New Shirt

Sam is a ___mechanic___ . He fixes _____ . Today he
           1   2

is at Shop Smart. He needs a blue _____ . Shirts are
                                          3

on sale. Brenda is a _____ . She sells _____ at
                            4   5

Shop Smart. How much is the shirt? It's _____ .
                                               6

3 Grammar

A Complete the sentences. Use *is* or *are*.

1. **A** How much _____**is**_____ the T-shirt?
   B $10.99.

2. **A** How much _____ the pants?
   B $28.99.

3. **A** How much _____ the shoes?
   B $39.95.

4. **A** How much _____ the sweater?
   B $22.95.

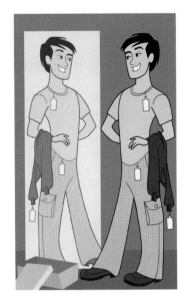

B Read and circle. Then write.

1. **A** Does Kayla count money?
   B Yes, she _____**does**_____ .
   ((does) doesn't)

2. **A** Does she clean buildings?
   B No, she _____ .
   (does   doesn't)

3. **A** Does Allen fix cars?
   B No, he _____ .
   (does   doesn't)

4. **A** Does he serve food?
   B Yes, he _____ .
   (does   doesn't)

4 Pronunciation

A Listen to the *e* sound, the *i* sound, and the *u* sound.

e	i	u
re*d*	si*x*	b*u*s

CD2, Track 33

B Listen and repeat.

e	red	when		i	six	his		u	bus	much

Talk with a partner. Say a word. Your partner points. Take turns.

CD2, Track 34

C Listen and check (✓).

	e	i	u		e	i	u		e	i	u		e	i	u		e	i	u
1.	✓			2.				3.				4.				5.			

CD2, Track 35

UNIT 9 DAILY LIVING

Lesson A Listening

1 Before you listen

A Look at the picture. What do you see?

B Listen and point: ■ doing homework ■ doing the laundry
■ drying the dishes ■ making lunch
■ making the bed ■ washing the dishes

◄) CD2, Track 36

UNIT GOALS
Identify family chores   **Interpret** a work order
Complete a chart about family chores

2 Listen

A Listen and repeat.

1. doing homework
2. doing the laundry
3. drying the dishes
4. making lunch
5. making the bed
6. washing the dishes

🔊 CD2, Track 37

🔊 CD2, Track 38

B Listen and circle.

1. (a.)    b.

2. a.    b.

3. a.    b.

4. a.    b.

Listen again. Check your answers.

3 After you listen

Talk with a partner. Point to a picture.
Your partner says the words.

Lesson B Outside chores

1 Vocabulary focus

Listen and repeat.

1. cutting the grass

2. getting the mail

3. taking out the trash

4. walking the dog

5. washing the car

6. watering the grass

2 Practice

A Read and match.

taking out the trash   washing the car   cutting the grass

1.

2.

3.

watering the grass   getting the mail   walking the dog

B **Listen and repeat.** Then write.

CD2, Track 40

Name	Chore		
1. Mrs. Navarro	_watering_	the grass	
2. Mr. Navarro	_____	the grass	
3. Roberto	_____	the car	
4. Diego	_____	_____ the trash	
5. Norma	_____	the mail	
6. Rita	_____	the dog	

Talk with a partner. Ask and answer.

A What is **Mrs. Navarro** doing?

B **Watering the grass.**

3 Communicate

Talk with a partner. Act and guess.

Watering the grass?

That's right.

1 Grammar focus: questions with *What*

QUESTIONS				ANSWERS
What	Is	he	doing?	**Cutting** the grass.
	is	she		**Walking** the dog.
	are	they		**Washing** the dishes.

👁 Watch

2 Practice

A Read and circle. Then write.

1. **A** What _____**are**_____ they doing?
   <u>is</u> (are)

   B Making dinner.

   A What _____ he doing?
   is are

   B Washing the dishes.

2. **A** What _____ they doing?
   is are

   B Making the bed.

   A What _____ he doing?
   is are

   B Taking out the trash.

3. **A** What _____ he doing?
   is are

   B Washing the car.

   A What _____ she doing?
   is are

   B Watering the grass.

Listen and repeat. Then practice with a partner.

🔊 CD2, Track 41

B **Listen and repeat.** Then write.

cutting   doing   drying   getting   making   taking

CD2, Track 42

1. ___Getting___ the mail.

2. _____ lunch.

3. _____ the grass.

4. _____ the laundry.

5. _____ the dishes.

6. _____ out the trash.

Talk with a partner. Ask and answer.

 A What **are they** doing?

B **Getting the mail.**

 A What **is he** doing?

B **Making lunch.**

3 # Communicate

Talk with a partner. Make a picture. Ask and guess.

What are they doing?   Drying the dishes.

Lesson D Reading

1 Before you read

Talk about the picture.
What do you see?

2 Read

Listen and read.

CD2, Track 43

● ● ●   Reply   Forward

From: Huan
To: Susie
Subject: Help

Dear Susie,

It's after dinner. My family is working in the kitchen. My daughter Li is washing the dishes. My daughter Mei is drying the dishes. My husband and Tao are taking out the trash. Where is my oldest son? He isn't in the kitchen. He is sleeping in the living room! I am not happy.

I need help. What can I do?

Huan

3 After you read

Read and match.

1.

3.

They are taking out the trash.

She is drying the dishes.

She is washing the dishes.

2.

She is not happy.

4.

4 **Picture dictionary** Rooms of a house

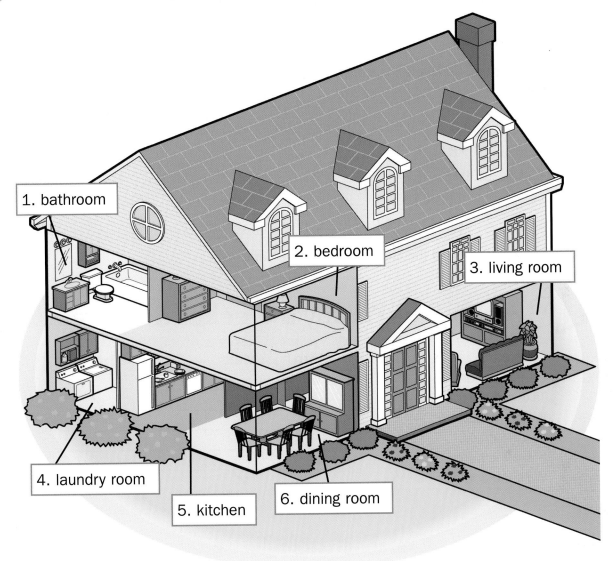

1. bathroom

2. bedroom

3. living room

4. laundry room

5. kitchen

6. dining room

A **Listen and repeat.** Look at the Picture dictionary.

B **Talk with a partner.** Point to a room and ask. Your partner answers.

 A What room is this?

B **The kitchen.**

 CD2, Track 44

Lesson E Writing

1 Before you write

A **Talk with a partner.** Complete the words.

1. d _o_ i _n_ _g_   t h e   _l_ a u n _d_ r _y_
2. m ___ k ___ n g   t h e   ___ e ___ s
3. w ___ l ___ i n g   t h e   ___ o ___
4. c ___ t t ___ n g   t h e   ___ r a ___ s
5. w ___ s ___ i n g   t h e   ___ i s ___ e s
6. t ___ k i n g   o u t   t h e   ___ r a s ___

B **Talk with a partner.** Read the chart. Complete the sentences.

Walker Family's Weekend Chores

Chore	Dad	Mom	Max	Iris	Charlie
Do the laundry.		✔		✔	
Take out the trash.					✔
Wash the dishes.			✔		
Cut the grass.	✔				
Make the beds.		✔			
Walk the dog.			✔		✔

It is the weekend. We are doing chores.

1. Charlie is ____taking____ _out_ _the_ ____trash____.

2. Mom and Iris are _____ ____ _____.

3. Dad is _____ ____ _____.

4. Max is _____ ____ _____.

5. Mom is _____ ____ _____.

6. Charlie and Max are _____ ____ _____.

2 Write

A **Complete the chart.** Write the weekend chores at your house. Write your family's names. Check (✓) the names.

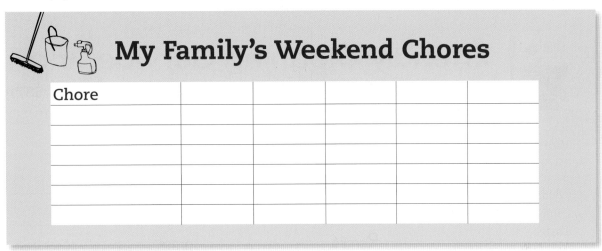

My Family's Weekend Chores

Chore					

B **Write.** It is the weekend. Tell about your family's chores. Look at 1B for help.

It is the weekend. We are doing chores.

1. I am _____ .

2. _____ is _____ .

3. _____ is _____ .

4. _____ is _____ .

5. _____ and _____ are _____ .

3 After you write

Talk with a partner. Share your writing.

Lesson F Another view

1 Life-skills reading

Friendly Cleaning Service, Inc.
We do your chores with a smile! Madison, WI 53714

Work Order for:
1812 Franklin Street

Madison, WI 53714

Date:
Monday, August 27

Name	Chore
Alma	dishes
Kay	beds
Ramiro	grass
Binh	laundry

Questions or Problems? Call Elena Sanchez at 555-1234.

A Read the sentences. Look at the work order. Fill in the answer.

1. What is Alma's chore?
   - (A) cutting the grass
   - (B) washing the dishes
   - (C) making the beds

2. What is Kay's chore?
   - (A) making the beds
   - (B) doing the laundry
   - (C) washing the dishes

3. What is Ramiro's chore?
   - (A) doing the laundry
   - (B) taking out the trash
   - (C) cutting the grass

4. What is Binh's chore?
   - (A) doing the laundry
   - (B) cutting the grass
   - (C) taking out the trash

B Solve the problem. Which solution is best? Circle your opinion.

Alma is sick. What should she do?

1. Call Elena.

2. Go to work sick.

3. Other: _____

2 Fun with vocabulary

A Talk with a partner. Complete the chart.

| the bed | the car | the dishes | the dog | the grass |
| homework | the laundry | lunch | mail | |

cut	wash	do	make	get
			the bed	

B Circle eight *-ing* words in the puzzle.

```
e  j  d  y  s  w  a  l  k  i  n  g  r  f  t
s  z  w  a  t  e  r  i  n  g  a  r  t  a  j
v  s  b  b  n  l  k  z  w  a  s  h  i  n  g
e  a  g  u  g  o  z  m  a  k  i  n  g  e  t
g  e  t  t  i  n  g  e  h  t  w  i  v  i  i
k  r  c  b  m  z  d  r  y  i  n  g  h  g  x
c  u  t  t  i  n  g  w  m  m  b  c  a  a  f
h  c  l  t  a  k  i  n  g  d  o  p  n  g  g
```

UNIT 10 FREE TIME

Lesson A Listening

1 Before you listen

A Look at the picture. What do you see?

B Listen and point: ■ dance ■ exercise ■ fish ■ play basketball
■ play cards ■ swim

 CD2, Track 45

Jane

Exercise Station

Dan

Jack

Lupe

UNIT GOALS
Identify free-time activities   Describe what people like to do
Interpret information on a class flyer

2 Listen

A Listen and repeat.

1. dance
2. exercise
3. fish
4. play basketball
5. play cards
6. swim

CD2, Track 46

CD2, Track 47

B Listen and circle.

1. (a.)    b.

2. a.    b.

3. a.    b.

4. a.    b.

Listen again. Check your answers.

3 After you listen

Talk with a partner. Point to a picture.
Your partner says the words.

Lesson B Around the house

1 Vocabulary focus

Listen and repeat.

CD2, Track 48

1. cook

2. play the guitar

3. listen to music

4. watch TV

5. read magazines

6. work in the garden

2 Practice

A Read and match.

| work in the garden | play the guitar | cook |

1. 2. 3.

| watch TV | listen to music | read magazines |

B **Listen and repeat.** Then write.

 CD2, Track 49

cook	listen to music	play the guitar
read magazines	watch TV	work in the garden

Name	Activity
1. Pablo	watch TV
2. Tom	
3. Rashid	

Name	Activity
4. Estela	
5. Ling	
6. Farah	

Talk with a partner. Ask and answer.

A   What does **Pablo** like to do?

B   **Watch TV.**

3 **Communicate**

Talk with a partner. Act and guess.

A   **Dance?**

B   **No.**

A   **Play the guitar?**

B   **That's right.**

Lesson C I like to watch TV.

1 Grammar focus: *like to*

QUESTIONS				ANSWERS		
	do	you		I	like	
What	**do**	they	**like to** do?	They	like	**to** watch TV.
	does	he		He	likes	
	does	she		She	likes	

👁 Watch

2 Practice

A Read and circle. Then write.

1. **A** What do they like to do?
   B They _____like_____ to play basketball.
   ⟳ (like) likes

2. **A** What does she like to do?
   B She _____ to swim.
   like   likes

3. **A** What does he like to do?
   B He _____ to play cards.
   like   likes

4. **A** What does she like to do?
   B She _____ to fish.
   like   likes

5. **A** What do they like to do?
   B They _____ to dance.
   like   likes

🔊 CD2, Track 50

Listen and repeat. Then practice with a partner.

B **Listen and repeat.**

 CD2, Track 51

1. exercise

2. cook

3. play cards

4. work in the garden

5. swim

6. play soccer

Talk with a partner. Ask and answer.

A   What **does he** like to do?

B   **He likes to exercise.**

3 Communicate

Talk with your classmates. Complete the chart.

A   What do you like to do, **Vinh**?

B   I like to **play basketball**.

Name	What do you like to do?
Vinh	play basketball

Lesson D Reading

1 Before you read

Talk about the picture.
What do you see?

2 Read

Listen and read.

 CD2, Track 52

●●●● LTE   1:20   100% ▮▮▮▮

< Messages   Lupe   Details

Hi Miriam,

I'm not working today. It's my day off. Are you busy? Come and visit me!

What do you like to do? I like to cook. I like to play cards. I like to listen to music and dance. I like to watch TV. Do you like to watch TV?

Please call me at 10:00.

3 After you read

Check (✓) the answers. What does Lupe like to do?

1.   2.   3.   4.   5.

☐   ☐   ☐   ☐   ☐

4 Picture dictionary Free-time activities

1. go to the movies

2. go online

3. shop

4. travel

5. visit friends

6. volunteer

A **Listen and repeat.** Look at the Picture dictionary.

B **Talk with a partner.** Point and ask. Your partner answers.

◀))) **CD2, Track** 53

  A What do they like to do?

B **Go to the movies.**

📖 Read a text message; use vocabulary for free-time activities UNIT 10 **129**

Lesson E Writing

1 Before you write

A **Talk with a partner.** Complete the words.

1. r _**e**_ _**a**_ d   m _**a**_ g a z i n e s
2. p l ____ y   b ____ s k ____ t b a l l
3. w ____ t c h   T V
4. v ____ s ____ t   f r i ____ n d s
5. ____ x ____ r c ____ s e
6. w ____ r k   ____ n   t h e   g a r d ____ n

B **Talk with a partner.** Write the words.

1. ___**exercise**___

2. _____ magazines

3. _____ basketball

4. _____ in the garden

5. _____ friends

6. _____ TV

2 **Write**

A **Complete the sentences.** Look at 1B.

My name is Brian.

Saturday is my day off.

1. I like to _____exercise_____ in the morning.
2. I like to _____ magazines, too.
3. I like to _____ basketball with my son in the afternoon.
4. I also like to _____ in the garden.
5. I like to _____ friends in the evening.
6. I like to _____ TV at night.

B **Check (✓).** What do you like to do on your day off?

☐ cook   ☐ play cards
☐ dance   ☐ shop
☐ exercise   ☐ swim
☐ fish   ☐ volunteer
☐ go to the movies   ☐ other: _____

Write about yourself.

My Day Off

My name is _____.

_____ is my day off.

I like to _____.

I like to _____.

I like to _____.

I like to _____.

3 **After you write**

Talk with a partner. Share your writing.

Lesson F Another view

1 Life-skills reading

Valley Community Center
Evening Classes
GUITAR CLASS
Learn to play the guitar.
September 3 to November 21
Monday and Wednesday
7:00 p.m. to 9:00 p.m.
Room 101
$100.00

A **Read the questions.** Look at the class ad. Fill in the answer.

1. What is this class?

   (A) a guitar class

   (B) an exercise class

   (C) an ESL class

2. Where is this class?

   (A) room 100

   (B) room 101

   (C) room 901

3. When is this class?

   (A) morning

   (B) afternoon

   (C) evening

4. How much is this class?

   (A) $10.00

   (B) $100.00

   (C) $101.00

B **Solve the problem.** Which solution is best? Circle your opinion.

Pablo wants to study guitar. He doesn't have $100. What can he do?

1. Talk to the teacher.

2. Save money and take the class later.

3. Other: _____

2 Fun with vocabulary

A **Talk with a partner.** Read and match.

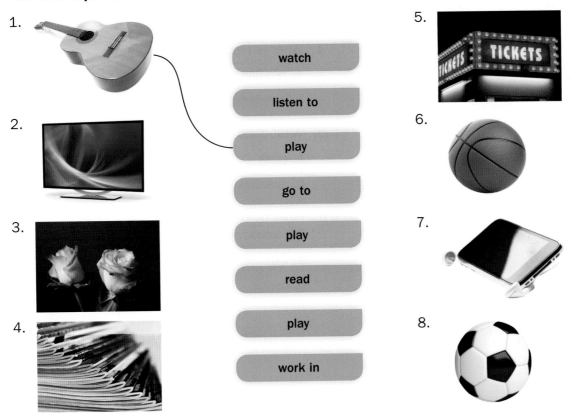

1.
2.
3.
4.

watch

listen to

play

go to

play

read

play

work in

5.
6.
7.
8.

B **Talk with a partner.** Complete the chart.

	Inside the house	Outside the house
cook	✓	✓
fish		
dance		
shop		
swim		
watch TV		

REVIEW

1 Listening

Read. Then listen and circle.

1. What is Marco doing?
   a. washing the car
   b. playing the guitar

2. What does he like to do?
   a. wash the car
   b. play the guitar

3. What is Ricky doing?
   a. making lunch
   b. making the bed

4. What is Fred doing?
   a. reading magazines
   b. watching TV

5. What does Tina like to do?
   a. cook
   b. exercise

6. What does she like to do on the weekend?
   a. fish
   b. dance

CD2, Track 54

Talk with a partner. Ask and answer.

2 Vocabulary

Write. Complete the story.

bedroom   kitchen   playing   watching   work

Sunday at Home

Today is Sunday. My son is ___watching___ TV in the living room.
                                    1

My daughter is _____ the guitar in her _____ .
                     2   3

My wife is in the _____ . She likes to cook. I am in the
                       4

garden. I like to _____ in the garden. Sunday is our
                        5

favorite day of the week. We like to relax.

3 Grammar

A **Complete the sentences.** Use *is* or *are*.

1. **A** What _____are_____ they doing?

   B Drying the dishes.

2. **A** What _____ she doing?

   B Taking out the trash.

3. **A** What _____ he doing?

   B Washing the clothes.

4. **A** What _____ they doing?

   B Getting the mail.

B **Read and circle.** Then write.

1. **A** What _____**does**_____ Pai like to do?

   do (does)

   B He _____ listen to music.

   like to   likes to

2. **A** What _____ Vance and Anh like to do?

   do   does

   B They _____ read magazines.

   like to   likes to

3. **A** What _____ you like to do?

   do   does

   B I _____ travel.

   like to   likes to

4 Pronunciation

A **Listen** to the two sounds of *a, e, i, o,* and *u*.

a	e	i	o	u
name at	read red	five six	phone on	June bus

CD2, Track 55

B **Listen and repeat.**

a	name	at

e	read	red

i	five	six

o	phone	on

u	June	bus

CD2, Track 56

Talk with a partner. Say a word. Your partner points. Take turns.

REFERENCE

Possessive adjectives

QUESTIONS			ANSWERS		
	my			Your	
	your			My	
	his			His	
	her			Her	
What's	its	phone number?		Its	phone number is 555–3348.
	our			Your	
	your			Our	
	their			Their	

Present of *be*

QUESTIONS			SHORT ANSWERS					
Am	I			you	are.			you aren't.
Are	you			I	am.			I'm not.
Is	he			he	is.			he isn't.
Is	she			she	is.			she isn't.
Is	it	from Somalia?	Yes,	it	is.	No,		it isn't.
Are	we			you	are.			you aren't.
Are	you			we	are.			we aren't.
Are	they			they	are.			they aren't.

Contractions

I'm	=	I am
You're	=	You are
He's	=	He is
She's	=	She is
It's	=	It is
We're	=	We are
You're	=	You are
They're	=	They are

aren't	=	are not
isn't	=	is not

Simple present

YES / NO QUESTIONS

Do	I	
Do	you	
Does	he	
Does	she	
Does	it	sell clothes?
Do	we	
Do	you	
Do	they	

SHORT ANSWERS

	you	do.
	I	do.
	he	does.
	she	does.
Yes,	it	does.
	you	do.
	we	do.
	they	do.

	you	don't.
	I	don't.
	he	doesn't.
	she	doesn't.
No,	it	doesn't.
	you	don't.
	we	don't.
	they	don't.

don't = do not
doesn't = does not

Present continuous

QUESTIONS WITH *WHAT*

	am	I	
	are	you	
	is	he	
	is	she	
What	is	it	doing?
	are	we	
	are	you	
	are	they	

SHORT ANSWERS

Working.

Simple present of *like to* + verb

QUESTIONS WITH *WHAT*

	do	I		
	do	you		
	does	he		
	does	she		
What	does	it	like to do?	
	do	we		
	do	you		
	do	they		

ANSWERS

You	like	
I	like	
He	likes	
She	likes	
It	likes	to swim.
You	like	
We	like	
They	like	

YES / NO QUESTIONS

Do	I	
Do	you	
Does	he	
Does	she	
Does	it	like to swim?
Do	we	
Do	you	
Do	they	

SHORT ANSWERS

	you	do.		you	don't.
	I	do.		I	don't.
	he	does.		he	doesn't.
	she	does.		she	doesn't.
Yes,	it	does.	No,	it	doesn't.
	you	do.		you	don't.
	we	do.		we	don't.
	they	do.		they	don't.

Simple present of *have*

YES / NO QUESTIONS

Do	I	
Do	you	
Does	he	
Does	she	have a sister?
Do	we	
Do	you	
Do	they	

SHORT ANSWERS

	you	do.			you	don't.
	I	do.			I	don't.
	he	does.			he	doesn't.
Yes,	she	does.		No,	she	doesn't.
	you	do.			you	don't.
	we	do.			we	don't.
	they	do.			they	don't.

AFFIRMATIVE STATEMENTS

I	have	
You	have	
He	has	
She	has	a sister.
We	have	
You	have	
They	have	

NEGATIVE STATEMENTS

I	don't		
You	don't		
He	doesn't		
She	doesn't	have	a sister.
We	don't		
You	don't		
They	don't		

Capitalization rules

Begin the first word in a sentence or question with a capital letter.	**M**y name is Nancy. **W**here is Ivan from?
Begin the names of months and days of the week with a capital letter.	**J**anuary **S**unday
Begin the names of countries, states/provinces, cities, streets, and other places with a capital letter.	**M**exico **F**lorida **T**ampa **P**ine **A**venue **T**he **C**lothes **P**lace
Begin the names of people with a capital letter.	**S**ara **G**arza **E**rnesto **D**elgado
Begin family relationship words with a capital when they are part of a name. Do not begin family relationship words with a capital when they are not part of a name.	I like **U**ncle Eduardo. My uncle is Eduardo.
Begin a title with a capital when it is part of the name.	**M**rs. Navarro **D**r. Martin

Punctuation rules

Use a period to end a sentence.	My name is Nancy.
Use a question mark at the end of a question.	What's your name?
Use an exclamation point to show emotion, emphasis, or surprise. It replaces a period.	It's Monday, your first day of English class! I love my family!
Use commas after the salutation and closing of a note, letter, or email.	Dear Grandma, Love, Meg
Use an apostrophe + an s to show possession.	the doctor's office = the office of the doctor Maria's son = the son of Maria a teacher's aide = an aide for a teacher

Cardinal numbers

0 zero	10 ten	20 twenty	30 thirty	40 forty
1 one	11 eleven	21 twenty-one	31 thirty-one	50 fifty
2 two	12 twelve	22 twenty-two	32 thirty-two	60 sixty
3 three	13 thirteen	23 twenty-three	33 thirty-three	70 seventy
4 four	14 fourteen	24 twenty-four	34 thirty-four	80 eighty
5 five	15 fifteen	25 twenty-five	35 thirty-five	90 ninety
6 six	16 sixteen	26 twenty-six	36 thirty-six	100 one hundred
7 seven	17 seventeen	27 twenty-seven	37 thirty-seven	1,000 one thousand
8 eight	18 eighteen	28 twenty-eight	38 thirty-eight	
9 nine	19 nineteen	29 twenty-nine	39 thirty-nine	

Ordinal numbers

1st first	11th eleventh	21st twenty-first	31st thirty-first
2nd second	12th twelfth	22nd twenty-second	
3rd third	13th thirteenth	23rd twenty-third	
4th fourth	14th fourteenth	24th twenty-fourth	
5th fifth	15th fifteenth	25th twenty-fifth	
6th sixth	16th sixteenth	26th twenty-sixth	
7th seventh	17th seventeenth	27th twenty-seventh	
8th eighth	18th eighteenth	28th twenty-eighth	
9th ninth	19th nineteenth	29th twenty-ninth	
10th tenth	20th twentieth	30th thirtieth	

Metric equivalents

1 inch = 25 millimeters	1 dry ounce = 28 grams	1 fluid ounce = 30 milliliters
1 foot = 30 centimeters	1 pound = .45 kilograms	1 quart = .95 liters
1 yard = .9 meters	1 mile = 1.6 kilometers	1 gallon = 3.8 liters

Converting Fahrenheit temperatures to Celsius

Subtract 30 and divide by 2.

Example: 80°F – 30 = 50; divided by 2 = 25

80°F = approximately 25°C

Countries and nationalities

Afghanistan	Afghan	Germany	German	Portugal	Portuguese
Albania	Albanian	Ghana	Ghanaian	Puerto Rico	Puerto Rican
Algeria	Algerian	Greece	Greek	Republic of	Congolese
Angola	Angolan	Grenada	Grenadian	the Congo	
Argentina	Argentine	Guatemala	Guatemalan	Romania	Romanian
Armenia	Armenian	Guyana	Guyanese	Russia	Russian
Australia	Australian	Haiti	Haitian	Saudi Arabia	Saudi
Austria	Austrian	Herzegovina	Herzegovinian	Senegal	Senegalese
Azerbaijan	Azerbaijani	Honduras	Honduran	Serbia	Serbian
Bahamas	Bahamian	Hungary	Hungarian	Sierra Leone	Sierra Leonean
Bahrain	Bahraini	India	Indian	Singapore	Singaporean
Bangladesh	Bangladeshi	Indonesia	Indonesian	Slovakia	Slovak
Barbados	Barbadian	Iran	Iranian	Somalia	Somali
Belarus	Belarusian	Iraq	Iraqi	South Africa	South African
Belgium	Belgian	Ireland	Irish	South Korea	Korean
Belize	Belizean	Israel	Israeli	Spain	Spanish
Benin	Beninese	Italy	Italian	Sri Lanka	Sri Lankan
Bolivia	Bolivian	Jamaica	Jamaican	Sudan	Sudanese
Bosnia	Bosnian	Japan	Japanese	Sweden	Swedish
Brazil	Brazilian	Jordan	Jordanian	Switzerland	Swiss
Bulgaria	Bulgarian	Kazakhstan	Kazakhstani	Syria	Syrian
Cambodia	Cambodian	Kenya	Kenyan	Tajikistan	Tajikistani
Cameroon	Cameroonian	Kuwait	Kuwaiti	Tanzania	Tanzanian
Canada	Canadian	Laos	Laotian	Thailand	Thai
Cape Verde	Cape Verdean	Lebanon	Lebanese	Togo	Togolese
Chile	Chilean	Liberia	Liberian	Tonga	Tongan
China	Chinese	Lithuania	Lithuanian	Trinidad	Trinidadian
Colombia	Colombian	Macedonia	Macedonian	Tunisia	Tunisian
Comoros	Comoran	Malaysia	Malaysian	Turkey	Turkish
Costa Rica	Costa Rican	Mexico	Mexican	Turkmenistan	Turkmen
Côte d'Ivoire	Ivoirian	Morocco	Moroccan	Uganda	Ugandan
Croatia	Croatian	Myanmar	Myanmar	Ukraine	Ukrainian
Cuba	Cuban	(Burma)	(Burmese)	United Arab	Emirati
Dominica	Dominican	Nepal	Nepali	Emirates	
Dominican	Dominican	Netherlands	Dutch	United	British
Republic		New Zealand	New Zealander	Kingdom	
Ecuador	Ecuadorian	Nicaragua	Nicaraguan	United States	American
Egypt	Egyptian	Niger	Nigerien	Uruguay	Uruguayan
El Salvador	Salvadoran	Nigeria	Nigerian	Uzbekistan	Uzbekistani
Equatorial	Equatorial	Norway	Norwegian	Venezuela	Venezuelan
Guinea	Guinean	Pakistan	Pakistani	Vietnam	Vietnamese
Eritrea	Eritrean	Panama	Panamanian	Yemen	Yemeni
Ethiopia	Ethiopian	Paraguay	Paraguayan	Zambia	Zambian
Fiji	Fijian	Peru	Peruvian	Zimbabwe	Zimbabwean
France	French	Philippines	Filipino		
Georgia	Georgia	Poland	Polish		

AUDIO SCRIPT

Welcome Unit

Page 3, Exercise 2A – CD1, Track 2

A, B, C, D, E, F, G, H, I, J, K, L, M, N, O, P, Q, R, S, T, U, V, W, X, Y, Z

Page 3, Exercise 2B – CD1, Track 3

1. Hello, my name is Anita. A-N-I-T-A.
2. My name is Daniel. D-A-N-I-E-L.
3. I'm Peizhi. P-E-I-Z-H-I.
4. My name is Yuri. Y-U-R-I.
5. Hi, I'm Franco. F-R-A-N-C-O.
6. Hi, my name is Lee. L-E-E.
7. Hello, my name is Hakim. H-A-K-I-M.
8. Hi there. My name is Karla. K-A-R-L-A.

Page 4, Exercise 3A – CD1, Track 4

1. Look.
2. Listen.
3. Point.
4. Repeat.
5. Talk.
6. Write.
7. Read.
8. Circle.
9. Match.

Page 5, Exercise 4A – CD1, Track 5

one, two, three, four, five, six, seven, eight, nine, ten, eleven, twelve, thirteen, fourteen, fifteen, sixteen, seventeen, eighteen, nineteen, twenty

Page 5, Exercise 4B – CD1, Track 6

1. six
2. eighteen
3. five
4. three
5. twelve
6. eleven
7. fifteen
8. nine

Unit 1: Personal information

Page 6, Lesson A, Exercise 1B – CD1, Track 7

area code, country, first name, ID card, last name, phone number

Page 7, Lesson A, Exercise 2A – CD1, Track 8

1. area code
2. country
3. first name
4. ID card
5. last name
6. phone number

Page 7, Lesson A, Exercise 2B – CD1, Track 9

1. **A** What's your area code?
   B 201.
2. **A** What's your phone number?
   B 555-5983.
3. **A** What's your first name?
   B Glen.
4. **A** What's your last name?
   B Reyna.

Page 8, Lesson B, Exercise 1 – CD1, Track 10

1. the United States
2. Mexico
3. Haiti
4. Brazil
5. Russia
6. Somalia
7. Vietnam
8. China

Page 9, Lesson B, Exercise 2B – CD1, Track 11

1. **A** Where is Ivan from?
   B Russia.
2. **A** Where is Asad from?
   B Somalia.
3. **A** Where is Eduardo from?
   B Mexico.
4. **A** Where is Elsa from?
   B The United States.
5. **A** Where is Luisa from?
   B Brazil.
6. **A** Where is Jun-Ming from?
   B China.

Page 10, Lesson C, Exercise 2A – CD1, Track 12

1. **A** What's your name?
   B My name is Nancy.
2. **A** What's his name?
   B His name is Chin.
3. **A** What's her name?
   B Her name is Alima.
4. **A** What's your name?
   B My name is Vincent.

Page 11, Lesson C, Exercise 2B – CD1, Track 13

1. **A** What's his first name?
   B Jack.
2. **A** What's his last name?
   B Lee.
3. **A** What's his area code?
   B 203.
4. **A** What's his phone number?
   B 555-9687.
5. **A** What's her area code?
   B 415.
6. **A** What's her phone number?
   B 555-3702.
7. **A** What's her last name?
   B Garza.
8. **A** What's her first name?
   B Sara.

Page 12, Lesson D, Exercise 2 – CD1, Track 14

Welcome!

Meet our new student.
His first name is Ernesto.
His last name is Delgado.
He is from Mexico.
Welcome, Ernesto Delgado!

Page 13, Lesson D, Exercise 4A – CD1, Track 15

1. January
2. February
3. March
4. April
5. May
6. June
7. July
8. August
9. September
10. October
11. November
12. December

Unit 2: At school

Page 18, Lesson A, Exercise 1B – CD1, Track 16

a book, a chair, a computer, a desk, a notebook, a pencil

Page 19, Lesson A, Exercise 2A – CD1, Track 17

1. a book
2. a chair
3. a computer
4. a desk
5. a notebook
6. a pencil

Page 19, Lesson A, Exercise 2B – CD1, Track 18

1. **A** What do you need?
   B A pencil.
   A Here. Take this one.
2. **A** What do you need?
   B A notebook.
   A Here. Take this one.
3. **A** What do you need?
   B A book.
   A Here. Take this one.
4. **A** What do you need?
   B A chair.
   A Here. Take this one.

Page 20, Lesson B, Exercise 1 – CD1, Track 19

1. a dictionary
2. paper
3. a pen
4. an eraser
5. a stapler
6. a ruler

Page 21, Lesson B, Exercise 2B – CD1, Track 20

1. **A** What do you need, Carla?
   B A dictionary.
   A Here you are.
2. **A** What do you need, Daw?
   B An eraser.
   A Here you are.
3. **A** What do you need, Stefan?
   B A ruler.
   A Here you are.
4. **A** What do you need, Felicia?
   B Paper.
   A Here you are.
5. **A** What do you need, Kim?
   B A pen.
   A Here you are.
6. **A** What do you need, Pablo?
   B A stapler.
   A Here you are.

Page 22, Lesson C, Exercise 2A – CD1, Track 21

1. **A** Where's my pencil?
   B In the desk.
2. **A** Where's my notebook?
   B On the desk.
3. **A** Where's my pen?
   B On the floor.
4. **A** Where's my dictionary?
   B Under the table.
5. **A** Where's my ruler?
   B On the table.
6. **A** Where's my paper?
   B Under the desk.

Page 24, Lesson D, Exercise 2 – CD1, Track 22

Sue,

It's Monday, your first day of English class! You need a pencil, eraser, notebook, and dictionary. The pencil is in the desk. The eraser is on the desk. The notebook is on my computer. And the dictionary is under the chair.
Have fun at school!

Mom

Page 25, Lesson D, Exercise 4A – CD1, Track 23

1. Sunday
2. Monday
3. Tuesday
4. Wednesday
5. Thursday
6. Friday
7. Saturday

Review: Units 1 and 2

Page 30, Exercise 1 – CD1, Track 24

1. **A** Welcome to class. What's your name?
   B My name is Hassan.
   A Your first name?
   B Yes.
2. **A** And what's your last name?
   B My last name is Ali.
3. **A** Where are you from, Hassan?
   B Somalia.
4. **A** And when's your birthday?
   B In August.
5. **A** What do you need, Hassan?
   B A notebook.
   A The notebook is on the desk.
6. **A** Ms. Garcia?
   B Yes, Hassan? What do you need?
   A Paper.
   B The paper is in the notebook.

Page 31, Exercise 4A – CD1, Track 25

/eɪ/
name

/oʊ/
phone

Page 31, Exercise 4B – CD1, Track 26

/eɪ/
name
day
say

/oʊ/
phone
code
note

Page 31, Exercise 4C – CD1, Track 27

1. say
2. code
3. name
4. phone
5. day

Unit 3: Friends and family

Page 32, Lesson A, Exercise 1B – CD1, Track 28

daughter, father, grandfather, grandmother, mother, son

Page 33, Lesson A, Exercise 2A – CD1, Track 29

1. daughter
2. father
3. grandfather
4. grandmother
5. mother
6. son

Page 33, Lesson A,
Exercise 2B – CD1, Track 30

1. **A** Who's that?
   B The grandmother.
2. **A** Who's that?
   B The daughter.
3. **A** Who's that?
   B The father.
4. **A** Who's that?
   B The grandfather.

Page 34, Lesson B,
Exercise 1 – CD1, Track 31

1. husband
2. wife
3. uncle
4. aunt
5. brother
6. sister

Page 35, Lesson B,
Exercise 2B – Class audio,
CD1 Track 32

1. **A** Who is Vera?
   B Sam's aunt.
2. **A** Who is Mike?
   B Sam's uncle.
3. **A** Who is Sophie?
   B Sam's sister.
4. **A** Who is Susan?
   B Dave's wife.
5. **A** Who is Sam?
   B Sophie's brother.
6. **A** Who is Dave?
   B Susan's husband.

Page 36, Lesson C,
Exercise 2A – CD1, Track 33

1. **A** Do you have a brother?
   B Yes, I do.
2. **A** Do you have a sister?
   B No, we don't.
3. **A** Do you have a son?
   B Yes, I do.
4. **A** Do you have a daughter?
   B Yes, we do.
5. **A** Do you have a wife?
   B No, I don't.

Page 37, Lesson C,
Exercise 2B – CD1, Track 34

1. **A** Do you have a sister?
   B Yes, I do.
   A What's her name?
   B Diana.
2. **A** Do you have a brother?
   B No, I don't.

3. **A** Do you have a husband?
   B Yes, I do.
   A What's his name?
   B Ken.
4. **A** Do you have a son?
   B Yes, we do.
   A What's his name?
   B Danny.
5. **A** Do you have a daughter?
   B No, we don't.
6. **A** Do you have a grandmother?
   B Yes, I do.
   A What's her name?
   B Rose.

Page 38, Lesson D,
Exercise 2 – CD1, Track 35
My Family

My name is Gloria. This is my family.
This is my mother. Her name is
Natalia. It is her birthday. This is
my father. His name is Enrico. This
is my husband, Luis. This is our
daughter, Lisa. This is our son, Tony.
I love my family.

Page 39, Lesson D,
Exercise 4A – CD1, Track 36

1. baby
2. girl
3. boy
4. teenager
5. woman
6. man

Unit 4: Health

Page 44, Lesson A,
Exercise 1B – CD1, Track 37

doctor, doctor's office, medicine,
nurse, patient

Page 45, Lesson A,
Exercise 2A – CD1, Track 38

1. doctor
2. doctor's office
3. medicine
4. nurse
5. patient

Page 45, Lesson A,
Exercise 2B – CD1, Track 39

1. **A** What's the matter?
   B I need a nurse.
2. **A** What's the matter?
   B I need a doctor.
3. **A** What's the matter?
   B I need a nurse.

4. **A** What's the matter?
   B I need some medicine.

Page 46, Lesson B,
Exercise 1 – CD1, Track 40

1. head
2. hand
3. leg
4. foot
5. stomach
6. arm

Page 47, Lesson B,
Exercise 2B – CD1, Track 41

1. **A** What hurts?
   B My head.
2. **A** What hurts?
   B My hand.
3. **A** What hurts?
   B My stomach.
4. **A** What hurts?
   B My foot.
5. **A** What hurts?
   B My arm.
6. **A** What hurts?
   B My leg.

Page 48, Lesson C,
Exercise 2A – CD1, Track 42

1. **A** What hurts?
   B My hands.
2. **A** What hurts?
   B My eyes.
3. **A** What hurts?
   B My arm.
4. **A** What hurts?
   B My foot.
5. **A** What hurts?
   B My legs.
6. **A** What hurts?
   B My hand.

Page 49, Lesson C,
Exercise 2B – CD1, Track 43

1. **A** What hurts?
   B My legs.
   A Oh, I'm sorry.
2. **A** What hurts?
   B My hand.
   A Oh, I'm sorry.
3. **A** What hurts?
   B My stomach.
   A Oh, I'm sorry.
4. **A** What hurts?
   B My feet.
   A Oh, I'm sorry.

5. **A** What hurts?
   B My eyes.
   A Oh, I'm sorry.
6. **A** What hurts?
   B My head.
   A Oh, I'm sorry.

Page 50, Lesson D, Exercise 2 – CD1, Track 44

At the Doctor's Office

Tony and Mario are at the doctor's office. They are patients. Tony's leg hurts. His head hurts, too. He has a headache. Mario's arm hurts. His hands hurt, too. Tony and Mario are not happy. It is not a good day.

Page 51, Lesson D, Exercise 4A – CD1, Track 45

1. a cold
2. a fever
3. a headache
4. a sore throat
5. a stomachache
6. a toothache

Review: Units 3 and 4

Page 56, Exercise 1 – CD1, Track 46

1. **A** Tom, who is Sonya?
   B My aunt.
2. **A** Tom, do you have a brother?
   B Yes, I do. His name is David.
3. **A** Ray, do you have a wife?
   B Yes, I do. Her name is Tina.
4. **A** Barbara, do you have a son?
   B Yes, I do. His name is Jay.
5. **A** What's the matter?
   B My head hurts.
   A Oh, I'm sorry.
6. **A** What's the matter?
   B My foot hurts.
   A Oh, I'm sorry.

Page 57, Exercise 4A – CD1, Track 47

/iː/
read

/aɪ/
five

/uː/
June

Page 57, Exercise 4B – CD1, Track 48

/iː/
read
need

/aɪ/
five
write

/uː/
June
rule

Page 57, Exercise 4C – CD1, Track 49

1. write
2. June
3. need
4. read
5. five

Unit 5: Around town

Page 58, Lesson A, Exercise 1B – CD1, Track 50

bank, library, restaurant, school, street, supermarket

Page 59, Lesson A, Exercise 2A – CD1, Track 51

1. bank
2. library
3. restaurant
4. school
5. street
6. supermarket

Page 59, Lesson A, Exercise 2B – CD1, Track 52

1. **A** Where's the school?
   B The school? It's on Main Street.
   A Thanks.
2. **A** Where's the restaurant?
   B The restaurant? I don't know.
   A OK. Thank you.
3. **A** Where's the library?
   B The library's on Market Street.
   A Thanks a lot.
4. **A** Where's the supermarket?
   B Sorry, I don't know.
   A Thanks, anyway.

Page 60, Lesson B, Exercise 1 – CD1, Track 53

1. pharmacy
2. hospital

3. laundromat
4. post office
5. movie theater
6. gas station

Page 61, Lesson B, Exercise 2B – CD1, Track 54

1. **A** Where's Minh?
   B At the movie theater.
2. **A** Where's Alan?
   B At the hospital.
3. **A** Where's Mr. Lopez?
   B At the pharmacy.
4. **A** Where's Paula?
   B At the laundromat.
5. **A** Where's Jackie?
   B At the post office.
6. **A** Where's Isabel?
   B At the gas station.

Page 62, Lesson C, Exercise 2A – CD1, Track 55

1. **A** Where's the pharmacy?
   B Between the restaurant and the supermarket.
2. **A** Where's the supermarket?
   B On Main Street.
3. **A** Where's the restaurant?
   B Next to the pharmacy.
4. **A** Where's the bakery?
   B Across from the restaurant.
5. **A** Where's the police station?
   B Next to the bakery.

Page 63, Lesson C, Exercise 2B – CD1, Track 56

1. **A** Excuse me. Where's the bank?
   B Next to the supermarket.
   A Thanks.
2. **A** Excuse me. Where's the restaurant?
   B Across from the bank.
   A Thanks.
3. **A** Excuse me. Where's the bank?
   B Between the pharmacy and the supermarket.
   A Thanks.
4. **A** Excuse me. Where's the police station?
   B On Park Street.
   A Thanks.
5. **A** Excuse me. Where's the bakery?
   B Next to the restaurant.
   A Thanks.

6. **A** Excuse me. Where's the supermarket?
   B Across from the bakery.
   A Thanks.

Page 64, Lesson D, Exercise 2 – CD1, Track 57

Notice from Riverside Library

Come and visit Riverside Library. The new library opens today. The library is on Main Street. It is across from Riverside Adult School. It is next to K and P Supermarket. It is between K and P Supermarket and Rosie's Restaurant. The library is open from 9:00 to 5:00, Monday, Wednesday, and Friday.

Page 65, Lesson D, Exercise 4A – CD1, Track 58

1. by bicycle
2. by bus
3. by car
4. by taxi
5. by train
6. on foot

Unit 6: Time

Page 70, Lesson A, Exercise 1B – CD2 ,Track 2

seven o'clock, nine o'clock, ten o'clock, ten-thirty, two-thirty, six-thirty

Page 71, Lesson A, Exercise 2A – CD2, Track 3

1. seven o'clock
2. nine o'clock
3. ten o'clock
4. ten-thirty
5. two-thirty
6. six-thirty

Page 71, Lesson A, Exercise 2B – CD2, Track 4

1. **A** What time is it?
   B It's nine o'clock.
2. **A** Excuse me. What time is it?
   B It's ten-thirty.
3. **A** What time is it?
   B It's two-thirty.
4. **A** Excuse me. What time is it?
   B It's ten o'clock.

Page 72, Lesson B, Exercise 1 – CD2, Track 5

1. appointment
2. meeting
3. class
4. movie
5. party
6. TV show

Page 73, Lesson B, Exercise 2B – CD2, Track 6

1. **A** What time is the appointment?
   B At one-thirty on Friday.
2. **A** What time is the class?
   B At eight-thirty on Friday.
3. **A** What time is the TV show?
   B At four-thirty on Friday.
4. **A** What time is the meeting?
   B At three o'clock on Saturday.
5. **A** What time is the movie?
   B At nine o'clock on Saturday.
6. **A** What time is the party?
   B At five o'clock on Saturday.

Page 74, Lesson C, Exercise 2A – CD2, Track 7

1. **A** Is your class at eleven o'clock?
   B Yes, it is.
2. **A** Is your appointment at twelve-thirty?
   B No, it isn't.
3. **A** Is your concert at eight o'clock?
   B No, it isn't.
4. **A** Is your movie at six o'clock?
   B Yes, it is.
5. **A** Is your party at four o'clock?
   B Yes, it is.
6. **A** Is your TV show at seven thirty?
   B No, it isn't.

Page 76, Lesson D, Exercise 2 – CD2, Track 8

Teresa's Day

Teresa is busy today. Her meeting with her friend Joan is at 10:00 in the morning. Her doctor's appointment is at 1:00 in the afternoon. Her favorite TV show is at 4:30. Her class is at 6:30 in the evening. Her uncle's birthday party is also at 6:30. Oh, no! What will she do?

Page 77, Lesson D, Exercise 4A – CD2, Track 9

1. in the morning
2. in the afternoon
3. in the evening
4. at noon
5. at night
6. at midnight

Review: Units 5 and 6

Page 82, Exercise 1 – CD2, Track 10

1. **A** When is the meeting with Mr. Johnson?
   B On Friday.
2. **A** Is the meeting at two-thirty?
   B No, it isn't. It's at ten-thirty.
3. **A** Is your appointment at two o'clock?
   B Yes, It is.
4. **A** Excuse me. Where's the school?
   B Across from the bank.
   A Thanks.
5. **A** Where are you?
   B At the movie theater.
   A Next to the supermarket?
   B Right.
6. **A** What time is the movie?
   B Seven-thirty.

Page 83, Exercise 4A – CD2, Track 11

/æ/
at

/ɒ/
on

Page 83, Exercise 4B – CD2, Track 12

/æ/
at
class
map

/ɒ/
on
clock
not

Page 83, Exercise 4C – CD2, Track 13

1. not
2. clock
3. at
4. class
5. on

Unit 7: Shopping

**Page 84, Lesson A,
Exercise 1B – CD2, Track 14**

a dress, pants, a shirt, shoes,
socks, a T-shirt

**Page 85, Lesson A,
Exercise 2A – CD2, Track 15**

1. a dress
2. pants
3. a shirt
4. shoes
5. socks
6. a T-shirt

**Page 85, Lesson A,
Exercise 2B – CD2, Track 16**

1. **A** How much is the shirt?
   B The shirt? $19.00.
2. **A** How much are the socks?
   B The socks? $1.99.
3. **A** How much is the dress?
   B The dress? $39.99.
4. **A** How much are the pants?
   B The pants? $24.99.

**Page 86, Lesson B,
Exercise 1 – CD2, Track 17**

1. a tie
2. a blouse
3. a sweater
4. a skirt
5. a jacket
6. a raincoat

**Page 87, Lesson B,
Exercise 2B – CD2, Track 18**

1. **A** How much is the tie?
   B The tie is $9.99.
2. **A** How much is the raincoat?
   B The raincoat is $26.95.
3. **A** How much is the skirt?
   B The skirt is $35.95.
4. **A** How much is the sweater?
   B The sweater is $39.99.
5. **A** How much is the jacket?
   B The jacket is $48.99.
6. **A** How much is the blouse?
   B The blouse is $25.95.

**Page 88, Lesson C, Exercise 2A –
CD2, Track 19**

1. **A** How much are the pants?
   B $24.99.
2. **A** How much is the skirt?
   B $18.99.

3. **A** How much is the raincoat?
   B $16.95.
4. **A** How much are the shoes?
   B $58.99.
5. **A** How much is the sweater?
   B $31.99.
6. **A** How much are the socks?
   B $5.95.

**Page 89, Lesson C,
Exercise 2B – CD2, Track 20**

1. **A** How much is the T-shirt?
   B $2.00.
   A $2.00? Thanks.
2. **A** How much are the shoes?
   B $3.00.
   A $3.00? Thanks.
3. **A** How much is the jacket?
   B $8.00.
   A $8.00? Thanks.
4. **A** How much is the sweater?
   B $4.00.
   A $4.00? Thanks.
5. **A** How much is the raincoat?
   B $5.00.
   A $5.00? Thanks.
6. **A** How much are the pants?
   B $6.00.
   A $6.00? Thanks.
7. **A** How much are the socks?
   B $1.00.
   A $1.00? Thanks.
8. **A** How much is the blouse?
   B $7.00.
   A $7.00? Thanks.

**Page 90, Lesson D,
Exercise 2 – CD2, Track 21**

Hi Patty,

This morning, Samuel and I are
going to The Clothes Place. Samuel
needs blue pants. He needs a tie,
too. I need a red dress and black
shoes. Dresses are on sale. They're
$49.99. Shoes are on sale, too.
They're $34.99. That's good.
Call you later,

Rose

**Page 91, Lesson D,
Exercise 4A – CD2, Track 22**

1. black
2. white
3. yellow
4. orange
5. brown

6. green
7. blue
8. purple
9. pink
10. red

Unit 8: Work

**Page 96, Lesson A,
Exercise 1B – CD2, Track 23**

cashier, custodian, mechanic,
receptionist, salesperson, server

**Page 97, Lesson A,
Exercise 2A – CD2, Track 24**

1. cashier
2. custodian
3. mechanic
4. receptionist
5. salesperson
6. server

**Page 97, Lesson A,
Exercise 2B – CD2, Track 25**

1. **A** What does he do?
   B He's a server.
2. **A** What does she do?
   B She's a receptionist.
3. **A** What's his job?
   B He's a custodian.
4. **A** What's her job?
   B She's a mechanic.

**Page 98, Lesson B,
Exercise 1 – CD2, Track 26**

1. She answers the phone.
2. She counts money.
3. He fixes cars.
4. He cleans buildings.
5. She sells clothes.
6. He serves food.

**Page 99, Lesson B,
Exercise 2B – CD2, Track 27**

1. **A** What does Sandra do?
   B She counts money.
2. **A** What does Stephanie do?
   B She serves food.
3. **A** What does Alba do?
   B She answers the phone.
4. **A** What does Oscar do?
   B He sells clothes.
5. **A** What does Tim do?
   B He cleans buildings.
6. **A** What does Ahmad do?
   B He fixes cars.

Page 100, Lesson C, Exercise 2A – CD2, Track 28

1. **A** Does he serve food?
   B No, he doesn't.
2. **A** Does he clean buildings?
   B Yes, he does.
3. **A** Does she answer the phone?
   B Yes, she does.
4. **A** Does he sell clothes?
   B Yes, he does.
5. **A** Does she fix cars?
   B No, she doesn't.

Page 101, Exercise 2B – CD2, Track 29

1. **A** Does he sell clothes?
   B No, he doesn't.
2. **A** Does he fix cars?
   B No, he doesn't.
3. **A** Does he clean buildings?
   B No, he doesn't.
4. **A** Does he serve food?
   B No, he doesn't.
5. **A** Does he count money?
   B No, he doesn't.
6. **A** Does he answer the phone?
   B Yes, he does.

Page 102, Lesson D, Exercise 2 – CD2, Track 30

Employee of the Month: Sara Lopez

Congratulations, Sara Lopez – Employee of the Month! Sara is a salesperson. She sells clothes. Sara's whole family works here at Shop Smart. Her father is a custodian, and her mother is a receptionist. Her uncle Eduardo is a server. He serves food. Her sister Lucy is a cashier. She counts money. Her brother Leo fixes cars. He's a mechanic. Everybody in the store knows the Lopez family!

Page 103, Lesson D, Exercise 4A – CD2, Track 31

1. bus driver
2. homemaker
3. painter
4. plumber
5. teacher's aide
6. truck driver

Page 108, Exercise 1 – CD2, Track 32

1. **A** Chul, what's your job?
   B I'm a cashier at City Café.
2. **A** What do you do, Chul?
   B I count money.
3. **A** Luz, what's your job?
   B I'm a receptionist at Shop Smart.
4. **A** What do you do, Luz?
   B I answer phones.
5. **A** Look! Pants are on sale.
   B What color are the pants?
   A They're blue.
6. **A** Excuse me. How much are the pants?
   B They're $19.99.
   A $19.99? Thanks.

Page 109, Exercise 4A – CD2, Track 33

/e/
red

/ɪ/
six

/ʌ/
bus

Page 109, Exercise 4B – CD2, Track 34

/e/
red
when

/ɪ/
six
his

/ʌ/
bus
much

Page 109, Exercise 4C – CD2, Track 35

1. red
2. much
3. his
4. six
5. when

Page 110, Lesson A, Exercise 1B – CD2, Track 36

doing homework, doing the laundry, drying the dishes, making lunch, making the bed, washing the dishes

Page 111, Lesson A, Exercise 2A – CD2, Track 37

1. doing homework
2. doing the laundry
3. drying the dishes
4. making lunch
5. making the bed
6. washing the dishes

Page 111, Lesson A, Exercise 2B – CD2, Track 38

1. **A** What's she doing?
   B She's doing homework.
2. **A** What's he doing?
   B He's washing the dishes.
3. **A** What's she doing?
   B She's making the bed.
4. **A** What's he doing?
   B He's making lunch.

Page 112, Lesson B, Exercise 1 – CD2, Track 39

1. cutting the grass
2. getting the mail
3. taking out the trash
4. walking the dog
5. washing the car
6. watering the grass

Page 113, Lesson B, Exercise 2B – CD2, Track 40

1. **A** What is Mrs. Navarro doing?
   B Watering the grass.
2. **A** What is Mr. Navarro doing?
   B Cutting the grass.
3. **A** What is Roberto doing?
   B Washing the car.
4. **A** What is Diego doing?
   B Taking out the trash.
5. **A** What is Norma doing?
   B Getting the mail.
6. **A** What is Rita doing?
   B Walking the dog.

Page 114, Lesson C,
Exercise 2A – CD2, Track 41

1. **A** What are they doing?
   B Making dinner.
   A What is he doing?
   B Washing the dishes.
2. **A** What are they doing?
   B Making the bed.
   A What is he doing?
   B Taking out the trash.
3. **A** What is he doing?
   B Washing the car.
   A What is she doing?
   B Watering the grass.

Page 115, Lesson C,
Exercise 2B – CD2, Track 42

1. **A** What are they doing?
   B Getting the mail.
2. **A** What is he doing?
   B Making lunch.
3. **A** What are they doing?
   B Cutting the grass.
4. **A** What is she doing?
   B Doing the laundry.
5. **A** What is she doing?
   B Drying the dishes.
6. **A** What are they doing?
   B Taking out the trash.

Page 116, Lesson D,
Exercise 2 – CD2, Track 43

Dear Susie,

It's after dinner. My family is working in the kitchen. My daughter Li is washing the dishes. My daughter Mei is drying the dishes. My husband and Tao are taking out the trash. Where is my oldest son? He isn't in the kitchen. He is sleeping in the living room! I am not happy.
I need help. What can I do?
Huan

Page 117, Lesson D,
Exercise 4A – CD2, Track 44

1. bathroom
2. bedroom
3. living room
4. laundry room
5. kitchen
6. dining room

Unit 10: Free time

Page 122, Lesson A,
Exercise 1B – CD2, Track 45

dance, exercise, fish, play basketball, play cards, swim

Page 123, Lesson A,
Exercise 2A – CD2, Track 46

1. dance
2. exercise
3. fish
4. play basketball
5. play cards
6. swim

Page 123, Lesson A,
Exercise 2B – CD2, Track 47

1. **A** Do you like to dance?
   B Yes, we do.
2. **A** Do you like to play cards?
   B Yes, we do.
3. **A** What do you like to do?
   B I like to fish.
4. **A** What do you like to do?
   B I like to swim.

Page 124, Lesson B,
Exercise 1 – CD2, Track 48

1. cook
2. play the guitar
3. listen to music
4. watch TV
5. read magazines
6. work in the garden

Page 125, Lesson B,
Exercise 2B – CD2, Track 49

1. **A** What does Pablo like to do?
   B Watch TV.
2. **A** What does Tom like to do?
   B Work in the garden.
3. **A** What does Rashid like to do?
   B Play the guitar.
4. **A** What does Estela like to do?
   B Listen to music.
5. **A** What does Ling like to do?
   B Read magazines.
6. **A** What does Farah like to do?
   B Cook.

Page 126, Lesson C,
Exercise 2A – CD2, Track 50

1. **A** What do they like to do?
   B They like to play basketball.
2. **A** What does she like to do?
   B She likes to swim.
3. **A** What does he like to do?
   B He likes to play cards.
4. **A** What does she like to do?
   B She likes to fish.
5. **A** What do they like to do?
   B They like to dance.

Page 127, Lesson C,
Exercise 2B – CD2, Track 51

1. **A** What does he like to do?
   B He likes to exercise.
2. **A** What does he like to do?
   B He likes to cook.
3. **A** What do they like to do?
   B They like to play cards.
4. **A** What does she like to do?
   B She likes to work in the garden.
5. **A** What does he like to do?
   B He likes to swim.
6. **A** What do they like to do?
   B They like to play soccer.

Page 128, Lesson D,
Exercise 2 – CD2, Track 52

Hi Miriam,

I'm not working today. It's my day off. Are you busy? Come and visit me!
What do you like to do? I like to cook. I like to play cards. I like to listen to music and dance. I like to watch TV. Do you like to watch TV? Please call me at 10:00.

Page 129, Lesson D,
Exercise 4A – CD2, Track 53

1. go to the movies
2. go online
3. shop
4. travel
5. visit friends
6. volunteer

Review: Units 9 and 10

Page 134, Exercise 1 – CD2, Track 54

1. **A** What are you doing, Marco?
   B Washing the car.
   A It's your day off! You need to relax.
2. **A** Marco, what do you like to do?
   B I like to play the guitar.
3. **A** Ricky, are you busy?
   B Yes. I'm making the bed.
4. **A** Fred, what are you doing?
   B I'm reading magazines in the living room.
5. **A** What do you like to do, Tina?
   B I like to cook.
6. **A** Tina, what do you like to do on the weekend?
   B I like to dance.

Page 135, Exercise 4A – CD2, Track 55

/eɪ/	/æ/
name	at
/i:/	/e/
read	red
/aɪ/	/ɪ/
five	six
/oʊ/	/ɒ/
phone	on
/u:/	/ʌ/
June	bus

Page 135, Exercise 4B – CD2, Track 56

/eɪ/	/æ/
name	at
/i:/	/e/
read	red
/aɪ/	/ɪ/
five	six
/oʊ/	/ɒ/
phone	on
/u:/	/ʌ/
June	bus

ACKNOWLEDGEMENTS

The authors and publishers acknowledge the following sources of copyright material and are grateful for the permissions granted. While every effort has been made, it has not always been possible to identify the sources of all the material used, or to trace all copyright holders. If any omissions are brought to our notice, we will be happy to include the appropriate acknowledgments on reprinting and in the next update to the digital edition, as applicable.

Key: Ex = Exercise, T = Top, B = Below, L = Left, R = Right.

Photos

All the below images are sourced from GettyImages.

p. 3: John Fedele/Blend Images; p. 4: Monashee Frantz/OJO Images; p. 5: Hero Images; p. 11 (L): Indeed; p. 11 (R): Nick Dolding/Stone; p. 14: David Lees/Iconica; p. 16: Katarina Premfors/arabianEye; p. 19 (1a, 3b): UmbertoPantalone/iStock/Getty Images Plus; p. 19 (2a, 4a): tulcarion/E+; p. 20 (Ex 2.2): Aleks_G/iStock/Getty Images Plus; p. 20 (Ex 2.3): fotodima/iStock/Getty Images Plus; p. 39 (baby): M-image/iStock/Getty Images Plus; p. 39 (girl): Emma Kim/Cultura; p. 39, p. 69 (boy & popcorn): Ljupco/iStock/Getty Images Plus; p. 39 (teenager): LWA/Dann Tardif/Blend Images; p. 39 (woman): davidgoldmanphoto/Image Source; p. 39 (man): Michael Blann/Iconica; p. 45 (Ex 2B.1a): Robert Byron/Hemera/Getty Images Plus; p. 45 (1b, 3a): iodrakon/iStock/Getty Images Plus; p. 45 (2a, 3b): Dan Dalton/Caiaimage; p. 45 (2b, 4b): leungchopan/iStock/Getty Images Plus; p. 45 (4a): Sezeryadigar/iStock/Getty Images Plus; p. 46: 4x6/E+; 47: gawrav/E+; p. 48 (1 eye, 2 eyes), p. 101: PeopleImages/DigitalVision; p. 48 (1 hand, 2 hands): s-cphoto/iStock/Getty Images Plus; p. 48 (1 foot, 2 feet): Valengilda/iStock/Getty Images Plus; p. 51 (cold): BJI/Blue Jean Images; p. 51 (fever): Jupiterimages/liquidlibrary/Getty Images Plus; p. 51 (headache): BSIP/UIG/Universal Images Group; p. 51 (sore throat): pablocalvog/iStock/Getty Images Plus; p. 51 (stomachache): delihayat/E+; p. 51 (toothache): Hemant Mehta/Canopy; p. 59 (1a, 4b): Steve Woods/Hemera/Getty Images Plus; p. 59 (1b, 3a), p. 129 (photo 1): andresr/E+; p. 59 (2a, 4a): Dave and Les Jacobs/Blend Images; p. 59 (2b): Cultura RM Exclusive/yellowdog/Cultura Exclusive; p. 59 (3b): Sam Edwards/OJO Images; p. 61, p. 113 (L): Morsa Images/DigitalVision; p. 63 (man): Nick David/Taxi; p. 63 (woman): Yiu Yu Hoi/The Image Bank; p. 65 (bicycle): GibsonPictures/E+; p. 65 (bus): Geography Photos/Universal Images Group; p. 65 (car): iPandastudio/E+; p. 65 (taxi): Waring Abbott/Michael Ochs Archives; p. 65 (train): Topic Images Inc./Topic Images; p. 65 (on foot): Dougal Waters/DigitalVision; p. 69 (envelope): patpitchaya/iStock/Getty Images Plus; p. 69 (money): H. Armstrong Roberts/ClassicStock/Archive Photos; p. 69 (towels): DonNichols/E+; p. 69 (medicine): fstop123/iStock/Getty Images Plus; p. 69 (popcorn): Ljupco/iStock/Getty Images Plus; p. 69 (bread): Fabio Pagani/EyeEm; p. 71: AlexRaths/iStock/Getty Images Plus; p. 77 (morning): IronHeart/Moment; p. 77 (afternoon): Antons Jevterevs/EyeEm/E+; p. 77 (evening): Iryna Shpulak; p. 77 (noon): Busà Photography/Moment; p. 77 (night): Charles Bowman/Design Pics/Axiom Photographic Agency; p. 77 (midnight): Ivantsov/iStock/Getty Images Plus; p. 85 (shirt, blue dress), p. 95 (pants, dress): rolleiflextlr/iStock/Getty Images Plus; p. 85 (shoes): turk_stock_photographer/iStock/Getty Images Plus; p. 85 (socks): kgfoto/iStock/Getty Images Plus; p. 85 (striped socks), p. 95 (socks): Dave King/Dorling Kindersley; p. 85 (red dress): Tim Ridley/Dorling Kindersley; p. 85 (pants): praethip/iStock/Getty Images Plus; p. 85 (t-shirt): vetas/iStock/Getty Images Plus; p. 85 (studying): shapecharge/E+; p. 86 (tie): NadyaTs/iStock/Getty Images Plus; p. 86 (blouse), p. 87 (raincoat): NAKphotos/iStock/Getty Images Plus; p. 86 (sweater): dendong/iStock/Getty Images Plus; p. 86 (skirt): Hugh Threlfall/Photolibrary; p. 86, p. 87 (jacket): popovaphoto/iStock/Getty Images Plus; p. 86 (raincoat): EdnaM/iStock/Getty Images Plus; p. 87 (tie): Photoevent/E+; p. 87 (skirt): Ratana21/iStock/Getty Images Plus; p. 87 (sweater): ersinkisacik/iStock/Getty Images Plus; p. 87 (blouse), p. 95 (sweater): ARSELA/E+; p. 95 (jacket): SteveCollender/iStock/Getty Images Plus; p. 95 (skirt): peangdao/iStock/Getty Images Plus; p. 95 (raincoat): Photology1971/iStock/Getty Images Plus; p. 95 (shirt): khvost/iStock/Getty Images Plus; p. 95 (blouse): lypnyk2/iStock/Getty Images Plus; p. 95 (shoes): Peter Dazeley/Photographer's Choice; p. 95 (tie): wwing/E+; p. 97 (1a): Jetta Productions/Blend (2a): ImagesBazaar; p. 97 (2b, 4b): kali9/E+; p. 97 (3a): kadmy/iStock/Getty Images Plus; p. 97 (3b): Images; p. 97 (1b): Fancy Yan/DigitalVision; p. 97 AndreyPopov/iStock/Getty Images Plus; p. 97 (4a): sturti/E+; p. 101: Frederic Lucano/The Image Bank; p. 103 (bus driver): tomazl/E+; p. 103 (homemaker): Jose Luis Pelaez Inc/Blend Images; p. 103 (painter): Photo and Co/Photolibrary; p. 103 (plumber): Blend Images - Jose Luis Pelaez Inc/Brand X Pictures; p. 103 (teacher): Caiaimage/Chris Ryan/OJO+; p. 103 (truck driver): ColorBlind Images/Blend Images; p. 107 (truck): mladn61/iStock/

Getty Images Plus; p. 107 (car): Rawpixel/iStock/ Getty Images Plus; p. 107 (cash register): Comstock/ Stockbyte; p. 107 (paints): Bob Elsdale/Stone; p. 107 (books): Moussa81/iStock/Getty Images Plus; p. 107 (telephone): Denis_Dryashkin/iStock/Getty Images Plus; p. 111 (1a, 3b): Photofusion/Universal Images Group; p. 111 (1b): CO2/The Image Bank; p. 111 (2a): Gabrielle Therin-Weise/Photographer's Choice; p. 111 (2b): Maskot; p. 111 (3a, 4b): McIninch/iStock/Getty Images Plus; p. 111 (4a): Jupiterimages/PHOTOS. com/Getty Images Plus; p. 113 (R): Caiaimage/ Sam Edwards; p. 123 (1a): monkeybusinessimages/ iStock/Getty Images Plus; p. 123 (1b): JackF/iStock/ Getty Images Plus; p. 123 (2a): i love images/Juice Images; p. 123 (2b): Tim Hall/Cultura; p. 123 (3a): Tiina & Geir/Cultura; p. 123 (3b): Johner Images; p. 123 (4a): Glow Wellness/Glow; p. 123 (4b): BraunS/E+; p. 124 (Ex 1.1): Gary Latham/Cultura; p. 124 (Ex 1.2): NanoStockk/iStock/Getty Images Plus; p. 124 (Ex 1.3): Dave & Les Jacobs/Blend Images; p. 124 (Ex 1.4): Robert Daly/Caiaimage; p. 124 (Ex 1.5): Manfred Rutz/The Image Bank; p. 124 (Ex 1.6): Amy Eckert/Taxi; p. 127 (exercise): DeanDrobot/iStock/Getty Images Plus; p. 127 (cook): Portra Images/Taxi; p. 127 (play cards): Jupiterimages/ Stockbyte; p. 127 (garden): Yellow Dog Productions/ DigitalVision; p. 127 (swimming): John Cumming/ Photodisc; p. 127 (play soccer): Westend61; p. 128 (T): Kelvin Murray/Taxi; p. 128 (Ex 3.1): Image Source; p. 128 (Ex 3.2): crossbrain66/E+; p. 128 (Ex 3.3): Maxim Pimenov/Hemera/Getty Images Plus; p. 128 (Ex 3.4): Michael Lamotte/Cole Group/Photodisc; p. 128 (Ex 3.5): malerapaso/iStock/Getty Images Plus; p. 129 (photo 2): Yuri_Arcurs/DigitalVision; p. 129 (photo 3): Paper Boat Creative/DigitalVision; p. 129 (photo 4, photo 6): Hero Images; p. 129 (photo 5): Ariel Skelley/Digital Vision; p. 133 (photo 1): Donal Husni/EyeEm; p. 133 (photo 2): selensergen/ iStock/Getty Images Plus; p. 133 (photo 3): Francesco Bittichesu/Photolibrary; p. 133 (photo 4): chris-mueller/iStock/Getty Images Plus; p. 133 (photo 5): YinYang/E+; p. 133 (photo 6): MicroStockHub/ iStock/Getty Images Plus; p. 133 (photo 7): Cagri Oner/Hemera/Getty Images Plus; p. 133 (photo 8): SonerCdem/iStock/Getty Images Plus.

Images sourced from the other libraries.

p. 19 (1b): Julia Ivantsova/Shutterstock; p. 19 (2b): zirconicusso/Fotolia; p. 19 (3a): Alfonso de Tomas/ Fotolia; p. 19 (4b): Tr1sha/Shutterstock; p. 20 (Ex 2.1): magicoven/Shutterstock; p. 20 (Ex 2.4): sagir/Shutterstock; p. 20 (Ex 2.5): Michael D Brown/ Shutterstock; p. 20 (Ex 2.6): CrackerClips/Stock Media/Shutterstock.

Illustrations

p. 2, p. 6, p. 8, p. 18, p. 22 (B), p. 23, p. 24, p. 25, p. 37, p. 40, p. 46, p. 47, p. 60 (Ex 1.6 , Ex 2.4), p. 61 (3, 6), p. 62 (B), p. 63 (4), p. 64 (T), p. 66, p. 71, p. 92, p. 100, p. 101, p. 112 (T), p. 113, p. 116 (Ex 3.1, Ex 3.3), p. 126, p. 130, p. 135: QBS Learning; p. 4, p. 49, p. 55, p. 61 (1, 2, 4, 5), p. 98, p. 124, p. 125 (B): Travis Foster; p. 7, p. 31, p. 36, p. 86, p. 88: Monika Roe; p. 9, p. 48, p. 112 (B): Pamela Hobbs; p. 10, p. 52, p. 109, p. 115: Frank Montagna; p. 20: Kenneth Batelman; p. 21, p. 34, p. 35, p. 114: Greg Paprocki; p. 22 (T), p. 26, p. 72, p. 87, p. 90 (B): Jason O'Malley; p. 57: Chuck Gonzales; p. 60 (Ex 1.1–1.5), p. 63 (1, 2, 3, 5, 6): Phil Williams; p. 60 (Ex 2.1, Ex 2.2, Ex 2.3, Ex 2.5, Ex 2.6), p. 99, p. 125 (T): Rod Hunt; p. 89: Greg Paprocki, Monika Roe; p. 13, p. 91: Victor Kulihin; p. 117, p. 133: Colin Hayes; p. 12, p. 32, p. 33, p. 44, p. 50, p. 58, p. 70, p. 76, p. 84, p. 90 (T), p. 96, p. 102, p. 110, p. 116, p. 122: Ben Kirchner.

Back cover photography by Hero Images; FangXiaNuo/ E+; pressureUA/iStock/Getty Images Plus; Adidet Chaiwattanakul/EyeEm; pixelfit/E+.

Front cover photography by Jetta Productions/Blend Images/Getty Images.

Audio produced by CityVox.